You Do Have a Voice

How to Unleash Your Inner Voice and Speak with Confidence

By

Serrinea Granville

For information: sgbookreviews@yahoo.com

ISBN: 978-1-7370630-4-9 (Paperback)
ISBN: 978-1-7370630-5-6 (AudioBook)

Imprint independently published.
November 2025

Dedication

To everyone who was ever told to be quiet,
to those still searching for their voice,
and to those who have yet to discover the power it holds.
And to my younger self—this book is for you.

Acknowledgements

First and foremost, I thank Jesus Christ, my Savior and Lord, for His guidance and strength. I give my deepest gratitude to my late grandmother, Esmin Granville, for always teaching me perseverance and determination. I am also grateful to my dear friend Shackera Bennett for helping me edit this book and for her continued support throughout this journey. Finally, I am also thankful to my manager, Y.Z., for your patience and understanding during the moments when finding my voice felt like the hardest thing to do. Your belief in me made all the difference.

Contents

Introduction

I was probably five or six years old when I first felt the sting of silence. I remember sitting among my classmates, their voices rising and falling as they talked and laughed together. I remember their laughter, the quick movement of their hands as they spoke. I wanted to join in, to share my little piece of the story. So I reached out, touched someone's arm, and just as I opened my mouth, I heard the words, "Be quiet, Serrinea. You talk too much."

It was a small moment, only a few words, but they stayed with me. They followed me. They pushed me into hiding. I built a closet inside myself, pulled the door shut, and locked my voice away. If I stayed quiet, no one could tell me I was too much. Too loud. Too unworthy.

If I stayed quiet, I wouldn't risk saying something that didn't matter.

I grew up, but the closet grew with me. It followed me into my twenties. By then, I was working in corporate America, dreaming of leading departments and climbing higher. On paper, I had everything I needed. In my head, I knew my work and my ideas were strong.

But when it came time to speak, my throat tightened. My ideas dissolved before I could share them. My voice fell low when I wanted it to be steady. My words stumbled when I wanted them to flow. I could see my future, but the very thing that was supposed to carry me — *my voice* — was the thing holding me back.

Maybe you know that feeling too. Maybe you've held back in a meeting because you didn't want to sound foolish. Maybe you've stayed silent with a friend or a partner because you didn't want to say the wrong thing. That was me.

For years, I thought silence would protect me. But silence also stole opportunities. It kept me small. *Invisible.*

Then something shifted. I realized I had a choice: keep shrinking into the background, or step forward and claim my voice. I had to reach down inside myself and say, *Serrinea, it's time to develop your speaking skills.*

And just like I did, you can too.

Speaking up is not a crime. It's the liberation of finally allowing yourself to be seen and heard. You only get one life, and you cannot speak up after the grave. So why not do it now? Why not let your voice out into the world today?

I know the fears that hold you back. Maybe you think your voice is too shaky, your accent too strong, or your words not polished enough. I thought all of that too. But what sounds awful in your head often sounds just fine to someone else.

This book is about realizing that everyone gets nervous. The speakers you admire— the ones who seem fearless—they get nervous too. The only difference is that they step into the spotlight anyway. They do it with sweaty hands, with racing hearts, with voices that sometimes quiver.

And if they can do it with a body full of nerves, so can you.

That is the promise of this book: to help you open the closet you may have shut long ago, the one that keeps your voice hidden inside. To remind you that the power has always been with you... and it is time to stop holding yourself captive.

The core of my reason for writing this book comes from everything I lived through as a child, teenager, and young adult. I know what it feels like to stay silent, to shrink back, to let fear of rejection keep you from raising your hand or speaking your truth. But I also know what it feels like to take charge of your life, to push through the fear, and to grow into someone who speaks with boldness. Signing up for Dale Carnegie training was a turning point for me, and to this day, having one of the most-viewed videos next to Warren Buffett himself remains one of my greatest accomplishments.

I share this not to boast, but to show what is possible when you choose to step forward. You have to take responsibility for your voice. You cannot wait for someone else to hand it to you. Staying quiet benefits no one but the enemy—it benefits those who prefer that you stay small and unheard. But speaking up? That shifts everything.

Too many of us carry old wounds into adulthood. Maybe a parent didn't model what it meant to speak with courage. Maybe someone shamed you when you tried to express yourself. But those experiences do not define who you are now. They do not control your future voice. Instead, they can become the very experiences that make you stronger, braver, and freer.

You have this one life to live. Make the best of it.

It's time to speak up.

Part One

Why We Stay Quiet

CHAPTER 1

How Self-Doubt Shapes Silence

I've learned that when something comes up in a meeting or group, there's a good chance someone else is thinking the same thing but doesn't know how to say it. You're not alone in your thoughts or hesitation. Many of us stay quiet out of fear of saying the wrong thing, when in reality, we're just waiting for someone to go first.

I remember several meetings, sitting around the table with managers and colleagues. Ideas were swirling in my head—ways to improve a process, suggestions that could help the team, even ideas that might have earned me recognition. But I didn't speak. I held back, quietly hoping someone else would say what I was thinking.

Why? For one, I worried about my accent. Coming from Jamaica, I spoke English, but not always the "proper" way that's expected in America. I feared no one would understand me. I feared public humiliation. Growing up in Jamaica, children were often told a well-known saying that they should "be seen and not heard." That message stayed with me. My palms would sweat, and nervousness would take over. In my mind, the audience seemed bigger than it really was. I would rehearse my words, correct them, and then shake my head, choosing to stay silent. I'd have entire conversations in my head: responses, agreements, questions, but they never left my lips. Inside, I spoke confidently, but outside, my voice remained hidden.

I watched as someone else spoke, sharing the very idea I had rehearsed in my head. They got the credit. The recognition. The moment I wanted. And I walked away thinking, *I could have done that. I should have spoken up.*

This fear didn't start at work. It followed me from all the way back in Sunday school and my early elementary school years, somewhere around grades four through six. I could never quite fit in with the other kids. I didn't share their sense of humor. I couldn't always follow the rhythm of their conversations. I felt safer around adults who showed me kindness than around my peers because speaking up with them often brought ridicule.

The fear I carried as a child (the fear of being laughed at, misunderstood, or dismissed) followed me into my twenties. In meetings, my heart would race just as it did in that Sunday school classroom.

These experiences, from childhood to the boardroom, taught me that self-doubt is not an innate feeling. It is learned. It is built from the voices around us and the messages we accept as truth. It can make your voice feel small, your ideas unworthy and senseless, your presence invisible. But understanding these roots is the first step toward reclaiming your voice.

<hr/>

Understanding Self-Doubt

To me, self-doubt feels like an emptiness, a hollow space where confidence should live. At its root, it comes from two places: not truly knowing who you are and not fully recognizing who God is or the strength and wisdom He has already placed within you. When we begin to see ourselves as He does, that hollow space starts to fill with purpose and peace.

Let's start with the first part: *knowing yourself.* If you really understood who you are, you would see that you are already a walking miracle. Think about it. You began as a single cell and from there grew into someone who can think, speak, move, and create. That alone is extraordinary.

Our minds have the ability to imagine what doesn't yet exist and then bring it into being; that's the creative and spiritual power we were given. That's the capacity we hold: to speak, to build, to create, and to influence the world around us. When we doubt ourselves, we forget that we were designed to make things possible, not just to dream them.

Think of it this way: if you place someone in a forest, they'll eventually learn how to live there. They'll find water and food, adapt to the weather, and grow

23

used to the sounds of the wild. In the same way, when you place your mind in the right environment, with the right people and the right kind of learning—your mind begins to adjust, grow, and thrive.

The mind has its own kind of muscle memory. Feed it what it needs, and it grows stronger. Train it constantly, and it becomes unstoppable. That same process applies to your voice. When you nurture it and keep speaking even when you are afraid (when your hands shake, when your words stumble a little), you are still building strength. Every attempt teaches you something new. With time, you begin to notice that you speak with a steadiness that once felt out of reach.

Knowing yourself is not about perfection or pretending to have everything figured out. It is about understanding who you are at your core and what shapes the way you think, speak, and respond to the world. Confidence grows from that awareness of yourself. It comes from standing in the truth of who you are, not who others expect you to be.

One reason we struggle to know ourselves is because of the voices we allow into our lives. The words spoken over us, especially when we are young, can become the truth we live by, whether they are real or not. If you grow up hearing, "Be quiet; what you say does not matter," those words can take root. And over time, your mind begins to believe them. You carry them with you, and they shape how you see yourself.

But the opposite is just as true. When you grow up surrounded by encouragement, hearing things like, "Your voice matters, what you say makes sense, and what you say can make a difference," —you learn to trust yourself. You begin to see that your ideas have power to shift perspectives and bring comfort to those who need hope or reassurance. To challenge and to inspire. Even if you did not grow up in that kind of environment, you are not trapped by the words of your past. Self-doubt may begin with the voices around us, but it does not have to end there.

Now let's look at the second part: recognizing who God is and the strength He had already placed within you. Self-doubt grows when we forget the source of that strength. As Ephesians 3:20 (KJV) states, "Now unto Him that is able to do exceedingly abundantly above all that we ask or think, according to the power that worketh in us." That same power already lives within us. When we fail to recognize it, self-doubt takes over.

Think about the moments when you've felt a pull to speak up in a meeting or share an idea, but fear rose in your throat and the words never came out. Your mind starts listing all the ways it could go wrong, and so you stay silent. Doubt whispered that maybe someone else was better for it. That pause isn't failure; it's a moment of forgetting the strength already breathing within you.

The truth is, self-doubt is not unique to you or me. It is a part of our journey. We can wrestle with a lack of confidence from time to time. That's normal. But doubt is not the destination. It's just a stop along the way to confidence.

The turning point comes when you realize that power has been inside you all along…your voice, your heart, your soul, ready to be recognized and released. When you begin to understand your strength and the strength God has placed within you, self-doubt starts to lose its hold. That is when confidence begins to take root and grow.

How Self-Doubt Shows Up in Communication

Self-doubt doesn't just live in your head. It shows up every time you try to speak. It finds its way into your body first. Your palms sweat. Your knees feel weak. Your heart races. You can feel it even before a single word leaves your mouth. I know these feelings well.

I remember sitting in meetings, ideas circling in my mind, solutions to problems, suggestions that could help the team, thoughts that could make a real difference. I would rehearse them over and over, only to stay silent when the moment came. My mind whispered, *Maybe it won't make sense. Maybe I'll sound foolish.*

I once worked with a woman who was brilliant at what she did. Her ideas were thoughtful, practical, and creative, yet she rarely spoke in meetings. When she did, her sentences always started with, "This might sound silly, but..." One afternoon, while we were struggling with a project, she quietly shared an idea she had been holding back for weeks. It was simple but exactly what we needed. The room fell silent for a moment, then everyone nodded in agreement. Afterward, she told me she had almost stayed quiet again because she was afraid of being misunderstood. Hearing her story reminded me of something important: so many of us hold back the very insight that could change everything, simply because we doubt that our voice is enough.

This hesitation isn't limited to work. It shows up in friendships, with family, even in casual conversations. You know what you want to say, but fear makes you pause. Fear convinces you that your words aren't important. You respond silently inside your head, imagining the conversation perfectly, while the real conversation passes you by.

Self-doubt also builds a comparison trap. You hear someone else speak, and they sound confident. They get recognition, nods, and laughter. And you wonder, *Why didn't I say that?* You forget that speaking confidently isn't about perfection. It's about letting your voice exist in the room. Self-doubt doesn't disappear overnight, but recognizing how it shows up in your body, your mind, and your voice is the first step toward reclaiming it.

Roots of Silence

The roots of silence are planted early — often through experience and messages we receive. It's like touching a hot surface as a child. Once it burns you, you remember to not touch it again. Speaking works the same way. Each time we try to speak and are met with ridicule, misunderstanding, or shame, we carry that memory forward. It shapes the ways we hold our voices; you learn to protect yourself by staying quiet.

For me, one of the first roots of silence was my accent. I worried that my accent would make people laugh or misunderstand me. I feared public humiliation. I remember one meeting where I tried to pronounce a word perfectly in my head, but I stumbled over it. In that moment, I retreated into silence again. I shut down.

Silence also grows from the fear that what we say doesn't matter, or worse, that our words might lead to embarrassment or public shame.

I remember Sunday school in Jamaica when I was about eight. I could never quite fit in with the other kids. I rarely spoke because I was afraid of saying something wrong. I had been told from early on that I talked too much, so blending in felt safer than being noticed. There was a boy I liked, and in my innocent confidence, I told him. I thought honesty would be something kind, something simple. Instead, he called over his friends. They circled me in the dusty schoolyard, their laughter loud and sharp, echoing in my ears. I stood there frozen, my face burning, wishing I could disappear.

That moment changed something in me. I learned that honesty could bring humiliation, that my words could turn against me. It wasn't about my accent then; it was about feeling small and unsure of where my voice belonged. I learned to feel safe hiding, safer with adults who would listen rather than ridicule.

What holds us back, too, is thinking too much about ourselves. We worry about how we look or sound instead of focusing on the message we want to share. We imagine an audience bigger and harsher than it really is. But audiences aren't there to judge; they are there to receive. They want insight, clarity, encouragement, guidance. They want something that helps them, their work, their lives, their communities. The more we focus on the purpose of our words, the less paralyzing self-doubt becomes.

We silence ourselves not only because of personal doubts but because of the ways we were conditioned to think about speaking. From childhood, many of us are told to "wait your turn," to "be quiet," or that questioning authority is disrespectful. Over time, those messages became ingrained. They create an inner voice that says speaking up is dangerous, even when no one in the room is trying to silence us.

Silence can also grow from our deep need for belonging. As children, being laughed at or dismissed by peers feels like rejection. Those moments plant seeds of fear: *If I speak, I might be excluded.* In adulthood, the setting changes from playgrounds and classrooms to boardrooms and meetings, but the fear remains the same. We hold back because we want to belong.

I remember in sixth grade, I had a crush on a boy in my class. I liked him so much, but I was too shy to say it out loud. Instead of finding the courage to speak for myself, I asked my friend Tashna to tell him for me. Tashna agreed, and I stood nearby, close enough to hear what he would say. His response cut deeply. He said, loud enough for others to hear, that he didn't want "that thing." His friends laughed, their laughter spreading across the room. The sting of their ridicule stayed with me long after the moment passed. To make matters worse, Tashna, the friend I had trusted to carry my voice, eventually began dating him.

That experience sealed something inside me. It confirmed what I had already begun to believe years before — that speaking up could bring pain. From that point on, I never told a boy directly that I liked him. Even if I felt it, I hid it because the memory of that laughter and rejection taught me that speaking up about my feelings could bring only shame and public humiliation.

Another memory that stands out is from my childhood birthdays. Mine is on January 4th, and I had a cousin whose birthday was January 3rd. His birthday was always celebrated, and one year, as a little girl, I thought perhaps I could share in the joy, that maybe we could celebrate my birthday too. I stood near the cake, smiling, hoping to be seen. But another child looked at me and said, "This is not your birthday. This is not for you." The words stung, and I learned then that putting myself forward, claiming space, could be met with rejection.

These moments may have seemed small to others, but for me, they became cornerstones of silence. They taught me that when I put myself out there, whether speaking, expressing feelings, or even celebrating myself. The response might be ridicule, dismissal, or exclusion. And so I carried those lessons into my early professional life, into my twenties, often holding back when it became time to speak up for myself or for the benefit of something greater than me.

Another layer of silence comes from cultural expectations. In some cultures, children are taught that modesty means not drawing attention to themselves. In others, accents and dialects are judged against a "standard." These unspoken rules shape the way we carry our voices. Speaking up can feel like betraying our roots or exposing ourselves to judgment.

And sometimes, silence is not only a fear but a choice. Over time, silence starts to feel familiar, even safe. We convince ourselves it protects us. Not speaking up feels safe. If we stay quiet, we will not be judged. If we never speak, no one can shame us. But that kind of acceptance is dangerous because it convinces us that hiding our voice is normal. Until we decide that silence is no longer acceptable, we remain trapped in it.

Here's the truth: most of the time, the audience is not waiting to critique. They are waiting to receive. They are not concerned with our accent, our mistakes, or the slight tremor in our voice. They want something for themselves: clarity, encouragement, insight, or even just honesty. And when we shift our focus away from ourselves and toward that purpose, silence begins to lose its grip.

The best speeches have never been about perfection. Christ spoke parables. He was not trying to be the perfect speaker; He spoke so that people could see their sins and move toward and accept salvation. As a result, His words echoed through generations.

That is the heart of impact, identifying the problems and clearly explaining the solution so that it reaches the heart and soul of the listeners. Marcus Garvey and Martin Luther King did not stand out because they spoke without error. Their words had purpose. They spoke with the goal of educating, liberating, and inspiring. Their audiences did not remember them for polished grammar or perfect diction. They remembered them because their words stirred courage, awakened hope, and moved people to action.

We, too, must shift our focus away from ourselves and toward the impact our words could potentially have. The purpose of our voice is not to make us sound perfect, but to leave something behind: an idea, an encouragement, a spark that makes someone else's life better. When we release the need to sound perfect, we free ourselves to speak with authenticity.

And being authentic is what connects most deeply with the audience.

So the challenge is not to silence ourselves until we are perfect but to step forward even when our words are imperfect, knowing they can still carry power. The impact of our voice lies in our purpose.

Silence is not just the absence of words; it is the presence of fear, memory, and belief. Every time we choose not to speak, we reinforce the idea that silence is safer than sound. That belief becomes a wall, one that grows higher with every unspoken thought. Yet walls can be torn down. And the first crack appears the moment we question whether silence should have so much power.

Breaking silence is rarely comfortable. It requires us to step out of the small shelter we have built and expose ourselves. There will always be risks in speaking. We may be misunderstood. We may stumble. We may not receive the response we long for. But there is also risk in silence. When we stay quiet, we lose the chance to be known, to shape conversations, to stand for what matters. Silence may feel like protection, but in truth, it erodes our presence until we no longer recognize our own voice.

Think of history again. Every moment that transformed the world began when someone risked breaking silence. One woman on a bus who refused to give up her seat. One young man standing before the United Nations. One teacher who told the truth in a classroom where no one else dared. None of them was a perfect speaker. They were simply people who decided that silence was no longer acceptable.

When we allow silence to dominate, we shrink the possibilities of our lives. We stay small in meetings, small in relationships, small in our communities. And that smallness does not serve us, nor does it serve others. Because the truth is, our words are not only for ourselves. They are for the person who needs encouragement, for the colleague who needs clarity.

Finally, silence grows from repeated external messages. If we are told repeatedly that our voices don't matter, that what we say is unimportant, it is natural to internalize those beliefs. But those messages are never the final truth. It is up to us, as adults, to decide whose voice we will believe. Our voice matters. What we have to say can influence, uplift, and leave a legacy. Understanding that is the first step to breaking free from the roots of silence.

It is easy to believe that silence protects us from shame, but it also withholds the healing that comes from being heard. When we speak, we invite connection. We invite change.

The roots of silence grow deep, but they are not indestructible. Every time we speak, no matter how small the moment, we loosen those roots. We choose to believe that our voice matters. We choose to step out of the comfort of hiding and into the courage of being seen.

And when we finally decide that silence is no longer acceptable, something shifts. We stop waiting for the perfect time, the perfect sentence, the perfect version of ourselves. We begin to trust that our voice, as it is, carries enough.

Because it does.

Reflection: Tracing Your Own Roots of Silence

Silence is never random. It has roots: experiences, messages, fears, and choices that shape the way we use or withhold our voice. To break free, we must first name those roots. Take a moment to think back to times in your life when you chose silence. Remember the setting, the people around you, and how you felt in your body. Ask yourself what kept you quiet. Was it fear of judgment, fear of being wrong, or fear of standing out? Writing these memories down will help you see the patterns more clearly.

Now, bring to mind the messages you grew up hearing about speaking. Maybe you were told to not talk back or that questioning authority was disrespectful. Perhaps you were encouraged to stay quiet, to wait your turn, or to keep certain thoughts to yourself. Those phrases, repeated often enough, can plant themselves deep inside. Naming them now is a way of loosening their hold.

Finally, choose one belief you are ready to shift. For example, if the old root was *If I speak, I will be judged,* the new root might be *If I speak, someone may be helped.* By putting that truth into words, you begin rewriting the story of your voice. Your silence once protected you, but your voice is what will free you.

CHAPTER 2

The Cost Of Holding Back

I remember one Sunday night at a youth convention. The church was full, about four hundred people gathered for the service. Each young adult was asked to say a few words in front of the congregation. I had prepared my part carefully. I told myself this was my chance to step forward, to come out of the closet within myself, and to show that I could be a public speaker someday.

When my name was called, I stood up and walked toward the front of the church. The pulpit stood ahead of me, slightly raised, with five steps leading up to it from the right side. I entered from that side, my palms damp and my knees unsteady. The congregation faced me from the left as I made my way up the stairs to the podium in the center. The lights above the stage felt bright against my face. In my mind, every eye in the room was watching me.

As I reached the podium, I became so aware of the audience that I could barely breathe. It felt as if their eyes were piercing through me as I stood there. Even though they were probably waiting patiently to hear what I had to say, all I could feel was their gaze. My mind drifted back to childhood, to the same

37

nervousness and uncertainty I used to feel when I wanted to be heard but was afraid of what might happen if I spoke.

There is nothing sweeter than a new voice, someone stepping out of their comfort zone and sharing who they are. I could feel that they wanted to hear me, wanted to know my voice.

But at that moment, I froze. I looked at the audience, and in my head, I thought I had nothing to say. The words I had rehearsed evaporated. I stood there for what felt like forever, staring out at faces that seemed miles and miles away.

Then, overwhelmed by fear and self-doubt, I turned and walked off the stage on the left side, opposite to where I had entered. I felt a wave of humiliation rise inside me. My heart pounded, and I wanted to disappear into the crowd. I was ashamed and convinced that my voice could not reach anyone, that nothing I had to say mattered.

It was a painful lesson. That moment, that lost opportunity, was the cost of holding back. I realized later that the audience had wanted to hear me, not judge me. But in my fear, I had silenced myself. That is what holding back does. It robs both you and the world of your contribution, your perspective, and your voice.

Missed Opportunities

Holding back our voice comes with real costs. One of the clearest is missed opportunities. These are moments that could have changed our lives. Professionally, personally, or even spiritually, but passed us because we stayed silent, focusing on fear instead of having faith in our God-given ability.

I remember one year when the Managing Director of a top bank in New York City called me into her office. She oversaw hundreds of employees and had built a reputation for recognizing potential in others. At the time, I was working as a Senior Analyst. She told me she wanted to promote me to an Assistant Vice President role, leading a team of my own.

I should have felt honored, but instead I hesitated. I turned it down. I told her I was not ready for the role. Deep down, it wasn't the job I doubted; it was myself. I didn't believe I could stand before a group and speak with confidence. I questioned whether anyone would listen or respect what I had to say.

I regret not accepting that role. I had always dreamed of becoming a Managing Director someday, and maybe that was the door that could have led me there. But the fear of speaking in front of senior leaders and the thought of others depending on my words made me shy away. That decision stayed with me. I must admit I regret that opportunity, which I now speak of not as a successful accomplishment but as a failed event. A moment when fear won. My confidence in my voice was low, and fear convinced me that I was not capable. I want you to pause and think for a moment. Have you ever been offered an opportunity and turned it down because you doubted yourself? Have you ever stayed silent when you wanted to speak, only to look back and wish you had said yes?

Missed opportunities appear in smaller moments too. Sometimes it is not volunteering an idea in a meeting, staying quiet when we could have resolved a conflict, or holding back from sharing an important thought with a friend or loved one. Each time we remain silent, we give up the chance to influence, to connect, or to create change.

The opportunities we miss by staying quiet can touch every part of our lives. Professionally, we may miss chances to grow, meet new people, or take on responsibilities that could expand our skills. Personally, we might miss the chance to connect with someone meaningful, to form friendships, or even find a life partner.

Holding back doesn't only affect us. It affects others. When we remain silent, we rob others of the chance to know the real gem we are. Many people have incredible personalities, insights, and ideas inside them, but if they never speak, the world never gets to experience them. By not sharing our voice, we hold back gifts meant to bless others.

Remaining quiet can also be ungrateful to God. He has given each of us a voice for a purpose. If we do not use it, it is like putting a precious gift in a corner, never dusting it off, never letting it shine. We were not given our voices to hide them away. They were meant to be used wisely and generously to impact our families, communities, and workplaces.

When you do not speak, you also diminish the collective power of a group. Think of the times you held back from suggesting a new idea or offering feedback in a meeting. By staying silent, you may have robbed your team of potential growth or missed the chance to make something better. Silence does not only affect you; it affects everyone who could have benefited from your words.

Some missed opportunities are easy to see, like passing on a promotion or holding back an idea. Others are harder to recognize, like the moments when we could have encouraged someone, spoken up for justice, or simply shared a truth that could have helped. Each time we remain silent, we risk regret. The longer we wait, the heavier that regret feels.

At the heart of it, remaining quiet robs us of opportunities. We are given the gift of speech, but by not using it, we withhold its power from the world. And one of the most painful consequences is regret. The missed opportunities and the unspoken words cannot be recovered, and that lingering "what if" is heavy, and it reminds us of the moments when fear outweighed purpose.

The Hidden Costs of Silence

Silence often looks harmless on the surface. To others, it may seem like simply being thoughtful, cautious, or respectful. But underneath, silence carries hidden costs that slowly change how we see ourselves. It lingers in our bodies as stress, tension, or shallow breathing, and it shapes how others experience us.

One of the first costs is the way silence feeds self-doubt. Every time we hold back when we have something to say, we reinforce the belief that our words do not matter. Over time, this becomes a cycle: the less we speak, the more invisible we feel, and the harder it becomes to trust our own voice. What starts as a moment of hesitation can grow into a habit of shrinking back and eventually into an identity of silence.

I noticed this in myself. In the beginning, when I first joined a new team, I felt out of place. I wanted to contribute, but I kept holding back. At first, I thought, *This is not right. I should speak up.* But the more I stayed silent, the more normal it began to feel. Eventually, it stopped bothering me as much, and silence became my default.

What I didn't realize then was that my silence was shaping not only how I saw myself but also how others saw me. To them, I became the quiet one. And the more I stayed quiet, the less people expected me to contribute. My silence became part of my reputation, and that was painful to recognize.

There were consequences. Being the quiet one made me feel like a weak link. I noticed that people overlooked me for opportunities, promotions, and even salary increases. Silence marked me as someone who could be passed over, even pushed aside. The habit of holding back didn't just affect how others treated me — it began to change how I valued myself.

The silence doesn't remain as a single moment. Repeated often enough, it becomes a way of life. It settles into your identity until you start believing that staying quiet is who you are, instead of what you've chosen.

One of my turning points came when I realized I couldn't make new choices without first looking back and beginning to heal. I had to return to the beginning and face what had shaped my fear. I remembered as a child being told to *shut up because I spoke too much.* Those words planted dark roots, shaping how I understood my own voice and whether I deserved to share it with the world.

It is a kind of deprogramming. You begin asking yourself hard questions. Why am I afraid to speak? Why do I tremble when I stand before a group? Why do I make the effort to speak, only to stop halfway?

That silence doesn't just stay in our minds. It settles into our bodies. The words we suppress create tension, like pressure building with nowhere to go. I remember times when I wanted to speak in a meeting but instead swallowed the words. My chest would tighten, my palms would sweat, and the moment would pass. Later, I would replay it in my head, wishing I had spoken. That cycle left me anxious and exhausted.

I once read about a study on workplace communication anxiety that found employees who regularly held back from speaking experienced higher levels of muscle tension, fatigue, and even insomnia. One participant described how, during meetings, his throat would tighten and his heart would race whenever he wanted to share an idea. This aligns with what trauma specialist Dr. Bessel van der Kolk writes in his book *The Body Keeps the Score* that the body stores emotional experiences, especially those connected to fear and suppression.[1]

In the end, silence showed up as stress, and stress became physical. The body keeps score of the moments we hold back, carrying the weight of unspoken words. It lingers in our posture, our breathing, and our stress levels.

Silence also affects our relationships. Words are how we connect, resolve conflict, and build intimacy. When we withhold them, misunderstandings grow. Friends may assume we do not care. Colleagues may think we lack ideas. Loved ones may feel distant, not because we do not love them, but because we never put that love into words. The gap between what we feel inside and what others see on the outside becomes wider with every unspoken word.

Silence doesn't just affect how we relate to others; it affects how we respond to God. The same hesitation that keeps us from speaking up in love can also keep us from answering His call. The servant of God, Moses, was a man who stuttered and shied away from public speaking. When God called him to lead His people out of Egypt, Moses tried to refuse. He had spent years leading sheep, a role that required little speaking, and now God was asking him to speak before a king. Moses must have remembered the embarrassment of his speech struggles, the way words caught in his throat, and how others may have ridiculed him. The thought of standing before Pharaoh, stuttering through every word, felt unbearable. So he said to God, "I am slow of speech and of a slow tongue" (Exodus 4:10 KJV). He believed his stutter disqualified him.

Do you understand that fear? How many times have you told yourself the same thing—that you are not the one qualified for the job, that your voice does not carry weight? Moses' silence nearly cost him his calling to lead God's people out of slavery. It is time to stop letting your silence rob you of opportunities. God does not call the perfect speaker; He equips the willing one. You may not be standing before Pharaoh, but you might be sitting in a meeting, standing in a classroom, or holding back from sharing an idea that could make a difference.

I experienced this kind of silence in the workplace. I would sit in meetings with ideas but remain quiet. The more I held back, the more I felt like an outsider. I began to believe I had nothing to offer.

Sometimes I whispered my thoughts to my manager and let her share them for me, hiding behind her confidence and her fluent speaking skills. It was my own version of Moses leaning on Aaron to speak for him. But over time, the cost was heavy. I stopped feeling like I belonged. I stopped growing. Eventually, I left the company, not because I lacked the ability, but because silence had trapped me.

Even as an adult, silence can feel like the easiest path, especially when facing authority. I remember having a very rude manager who would constantly criticize our work and dismiss our efforts. No matter how hard we tried, it never seemed enough. For a long time, I stayed quiet, letting her words overshadow my own voice.

But there came a moment when I realized that waiting for someone else to speak for me wasn't enough. Respectfully, I stepped forward and said, "I don't agree with your comments. We are giving our best efforts, and this work is difficult, but we are committed to making it right."

It was a revelation. Just like running a race, no one can run it for you. The fastest man alive could not have sent someone else to win in his place. In life, we have a responsibility to advocate for ourselves. Speaking up doesn't just protect our dignity. It allows us to fulfill our potential, to impact those around us, and to live fully. That day, I learned that silence may feel safe, but courage brings freedom.

And silence does not only carry mental, physical, and emotional costs. There is also a spiritual cost. God gave us a voice for a reason. When we do not use it, it is like leaving a precious gift unopened. Our silence is not neutral. It is wasteful. To stay silent is, in a way, to overlook the gift God has placed within us.

---

[1] Insight adapted from Dr. Bessel van der Kolk's book The Body Keeps the Score (Penguin Books, 2015), which explains how the body holds emotional and psychological stress over time.

Reframing Silence

After understanding the many costs of silence, the next question becomes, what do we do with it? How do we know when silence is protecting us and when it is holding us back? My belief is that the answer begins with purpose.

I often ask myself, *What is the reason I want to speak right now?* If my words can bring clarity, encouragement, or even healing to someone else, then silence is not my friend. Think about leaders like Martin Luther King Jr. or Nelson Mandela. They faced fear, opposition, and danger, yet their words carried purpose. They weren't speaking just to hear themselves talk. They did not speak just to be heard; they spoke to serve, to guide, and to transform lives.

In smaller ways, we each face that same choice. Maybe we are in a meeting at work and have an idea that could make things better for the team. Maybe we are with a friend who is hurting, and we feel the urge to share a story that might comfort them. Maybe we are at church or at a family gathering, and an encouraging thought comes to mind. In those moments, silence may feel safer, but if our words could help someone, then holding back is not protection. It is a loss, for us and for them.

Not every word needs to be spoken. Sometimes silence is wisdom. If the words I am about to say come from pride, frustration, or the need to be right, speaking them would only add noise, not value. In those moments, silence protects peace. But if I stay quiet out of fear (fear of judgment, of being misunderstood, or of not being respected), that silence does not serve me. It shrinks me.

So how do we know the difference? It starts with intention. Ask yourself: *Am I staying silent to protect peace or to protect fear?* If your silence brings calm, clarity, or safety, it is wisdom. If it brings regret, tension, or a sense of smallness, it is fear.

In real time, it can be difficult to discern whether our silence comes from fear or wisdom. That is why practice matters. Each time we take the risk to speak, we learn more about ourselves and how we respond under pressure. When we ignore fear and choose to speak, we begin to see that the world does not fall apart. We discover that our voice can be heard, that we can recover from mistakes, and that life continues even after a moment of nervousness or a speech that did not go as planned.

We also experience the joy of when our words create impact and connect with the audience. When someone nods in understanding or thanks us. And sometimes we learn by missteps too, by saying too much, or saying it at the wrong time. When silence would have served better. But even then, we grow. Those moments become teachers.

What matters most is the beginning. We will never discover the balance between fear and wisdom by staying silent. We discover it by speaking, by testing our voice in small moments, and by noticing how it feels and what it creates. Over time, that awareness becomes discernment, an inner sense of knowing how to read the room.

I experienced this firsthand after completing a public speaking training course. Just a week later, I went into a restaurant, and something simple became a test. Normally, I would have been asked several times what I wanted because my voice was so soft. Inside, I felt small, and outside, I sounded small. But that day I decided to practice what I had learned: speak firmly and louder than I thought I needed to. When I gave my order, the man in front of me actually turned and said, "Wow, you speak so powerfully." That moment showed me how different I could sound simply by stepping out of myself and applying what I'd practiced. By stepping into confidence.

I have also noticed something else. When I speak up from a place of purpose, even if my voice shakes, I feel free. The fear loosens its grip. My chest feels lighter. My mind feels clearer. Sometimes the very act of speaking is what reminds me that I am more capable than my fear tells me I am. In those moments, silence is the enemy, and speaking up is my ally.

Reframing silence, then, is not about choosing to speak all the time. It is about choosing with awareness. It is about asking, "Will my silence protect or limit me? Will my words harm or help?" When our answer points toward growth, service, or love, then our voices are needed.

This is not something we master in one day. It is something we learn as we go, one word, one choice at a time. And it all begins with giving ourselves permission to speak, to practice, and to discover who we are when our voice is finally heard.

Reflection: Noticing Your Silence

Take a moment to think about last week. Were there times when you wanted to speak up but stayed quiet? Maybe at work, with friends, or with family? Try to recall the exact moments, the feelings in your body, and what stopped you from speaking.

Now, consider the consequences. Did staying silent affect your relationships, your confidence, or even your sense of purpose? Write down a few examples in a notebook. This is not about criticizing yourself. It is about observing patterns and understanding where your silence shows up.

Next, choose one small moment in the coming week to test your voice. It could be sharing an idea in a meeting, giving a compliment, or simply stating your preference when asked. Notice how it feels in your body before, during, and after speaking. Do you feel lighter, relieved, or proud? Reflect on that experience in writing.

The goal is not to force yourself to speak all the time. The goal is to begin recognizing when silence protects and when it is holding you back. By observing your habits, testing your voice, and reflecting on the impact, you begin the practice of reclaiming your presence. One moment, one word, and one choice at a time.

Part Two

Preparing to Speak

CHAPTER 3

Rewriting Your Inner Dialogue

For a long time, I didn't truly recognize my inner voice. It was there, quietly influencing my choices, but I didn't give it the recognition it deserved. I didn't stop to consider how much power it had in shaping my thoughts and directing my days. I let it guide me without questioning where it came from, what exactly it was saying, or, most importantly, where it was leading me. Most of the time, it whispered doubt: *You don't belong. Your words don't matter. Stay quiet.* And I believed it.

Looking back, it was like driving a car every day without ever checking the health of the engine. I never stopped to see if it needed attention, if it was running smoothly, or where it might break down. In the same way, I didn't stop to examine my inner voice to see if it was guiding me in the right direction or if its core beliefs were feeding me truth or negativity. I never "serviced" it. So, just like a neglected engine, my inner voice kept running on autopilot, powered by untested and unhealthy thoughts. And because those thoughts were often negative, my life followed their lead: shrinking back, staying silent, and letting others speak for me.

In meetings at work, I would write down notes and pass them to my manager or whisper my ideas for her to share. I felt safer standing behind someone else's voice than using my own because I hadn't yet realized I carried a power source within me called an "inner voice."

The truth is, our inner dialogue shapes everything. The Bible says, "Out of the abundance of the heart, the mouth speaks" (Matthew 12:34 KJV). What we believe in our hearts, what that inner voice repeats, eventually shows up in our actions and in our silence. During that season of my life, my heart was heavy with doubt, self-pity, and weakness. My inner voice even comforted me in my negative beliefs. It told me it was okay to be a horrible speaker, okay to let others laugh, okay to stay hidden and do nothing about it because I convinced myself I would never be good enough.

But here's what I've learned: the inner voice is not fixed. It is like a child that has to be taught, guided, and nurtured. Left alone, it may grow wild and negative, but with care, it can be trained to tell us the truth: to speak of possibility, courage, and hope.

This chapter is about that shift. It is about learning to recognize the voice inside you and beginning the work of rewriting the dialogue so it no longer holds you back but instead leads you forward.

Recognizing the Default Voice

Most of us go through life without even noticing the constant stream of self-talk running in the background. It is like a radio playing in another room, always on, shaping how we feel, how we act, and how we see ourselves. The problem is, whatever we sow into our inner voice from our life experiences is what remains and eventually becomes what we reap. If, growing up, you were often told you were a poor speaker, or if your experiences taught you that speaking up rarely led to good results, those messages become the soundtrack of your inner voice. Over time, the constant repetition of those memories and words builds a belief system rooted in failure. And when we don't pay attention to that inner dialogue, it begins to run our lives on its own. The voice defaults to negativity. It tells us we don't belong, that we have nothing to contribute, and that staying quiet is safer.

For me, my default inner voice lacked confidence and energy. I had no belief in myself, which aligned perfectly with what my inner voice was already saying. I thought that my lack of confidence in speaking was simply who I was. That it was part of my nature and that no improvement could ever be made. When I said, "I'm the worst speaker in the world," I believed it. From an early age, I absorbed the idea that I should stay quiet, that nothing good would come from speaking up. My inner voice became the seed of that belief: weak, negative, and unchallenged. I accepted it without question, and that acceptance shaped my choices.

I decided it was better to stay quiet. It felt safer to stand behind others who seemed confident and spoke with ease. Whenever someone used their voice beautifully, my inner voice would whisper, *That's amazing. I could never do that.* And I believed it.

That voice followed me into my career. At the time, I was working at a major bank in New York City, and I had been holding back for so long that silence felt normal. When my senior manager called me into her office one afternoon, she told me she had noticed that I rarely spoke during meetings. She said I had good ideas, but that I often let my direct manager speak for me. She wanted me to take the lead in client meetings and share my thoughts directly. But the moment she said it, I froze. My tongue felt tied. Inside, I told myself I had nothing valuable to offer, no ideas worth sharing. That belief kept me silent, but the silence started to haunt me.

I remember sleepless nights, lying awake, replaying meetings in my mind. I began to notice the pattern: every time I stayed quiet, I reinforced the thought that I was invisible, that I had nothing to give. Deep down, a small part of me knew that was not true, but the default voice was louder. It told me I was weak in confidence and in presence. It convinced me that speaking would only expose my flaws and prove that I didn't belong.

When the company shifted managers on our team, Mr. U became my new supervisor. Things quickly grew more difficult. One day, he looked at me with folded arms and asked to see my college diploma. He doubted that I even belonged in the role. And why? Because I was not speaking, or most times when I tried, the words came out as faint mutters no one could understand. I was doing the repetitive parts of the job, but my silence made me look like an empty chair in the room. To him, and maybe to others, I looked like an imposter.

What made that moment even more painful was the humiliation I felt. Mr. U was a light-skinned man, and when he questioned my college qualifications, I felt as though I had let down my own race. I carried the weight of that moment as if my silence had confirmed his doubt. It wasn't just professional shame. It was personal. And for the first time, I saw the truth: I needed to feed that inner voice something different — training, practice, and encouragement. That was the only way forward.

Awareness was the first step. Simply noticing that the voice in my head existed and that it was not telling me the truth opened the door to change. Without awareness, nothing shifts. With it, everything can. Awareness always begins small. You don't need to silence every thought or completely change your inner language overnight. What you need is to begin noticing. Many of us move through the day without ever stopping to ask, *What am I saying to myself right now?* Those words are often quiet, automatic, and so familiar that they often slip past our notice.

The first step is to pause. The next time you feel nervous before a meeting, frustrated after a conversation, or doubtful about taking a chance, catch yourself in that exact moment. Ask, *What did my mind just say? Did it encourage me or shut me down?*

You may find that your inner dialogue is filled with old phrases you've repeated for years: I'm not ready. I'll sound foolish. I have nothing new to add. That's your default voice at work. Recognizing it doesn't mean judging yourself. It means observing, as if you were listening in on someone else's conversation.

From there, you can begin the practice of writing these thoughts down. Putting them on paper makes them visible, almost tangible, and creates space between you and them. That distance is where change begins. Because once you see your inner dialogue clearly, you can begin to ask, *Is this helping me? Or is this holding me back?*

Interrupting the Script

Once I recognized that my default voice was not helping me, the next step was to interrupt it. I had to stop letting that negative dialogue run on autopilot and start creating a new script.

I remember sitting down with a piece of paper and writing out what I really wanted for my life. At the top of the list was a dream: owning my own company. But when I looked at that dream, I realized something important. No business can survive without communication. I could not run a company without talking to vendors, connecting with clients, or leading a team. Every leader must be able to speak publicly: to inspire staff, share their vision, and represent their organization with confidence. If I stayed silent, the dream would die before it even started.

So I made communication my priority. Training was part of the process, but the real transformation came from changing my mindset. I had to begin taking intentional risks — raising my hand even when I wasn't sure I had the perfect answer, asking questions that might seem obvious, and volunteering for opportunities that made my stomach churn. Each small leap tested my limits, and even when I fell short, when I stumbled, I discovered I could recover.

That resilience was more valuable than getting everything right the first time. If I was an imposter, then eventually people would find out. So what was the worst that could happen? Maybe I would fail. Maybe they would let me go. But if I tried, at least I would know I had taken my shot. That decision empowered me to step forward, even if I wasn't perfect.

I began small. I practiced speaking up a little in meetings, even if it was just a sentence or two. I stumbled, I stammered, and sometimes my manager had to rephrase what I meant. But every attempt was progress. I was interrupting the old script that told me to stay silent and allowing a new voice to take shape.

I also built rituals around speaking. I stood in front of the mirror, looked myself in the eyes, and spoke affirmations:

★ I am a strong speaker.
★ I am bold.
★ I am a creative thinker.

I used my hands while I spoke because movement gave my words energy and confidence.

Here is something powerful: practice with people who love you enough to be honest. If you have children, speak in front of them. A child will tell you the truth. I practiced with friends because honesty, when given in love, helps you grow. And I gave myself a promise: in every group I was part of—at work, at church, or in professional circles—I would speak at least once. Even if it was small. Even if it was just a few words. Even if it was imperfect.

What you'll find is that these little experiments build momentum. Volunteering to share in a group, reading aloud at church, raising your hand at work are all forms of practice.

Interrupting the script is not just about forcing yourself to talk. It is about creating a new pattern in your mind. Neuroscience shows that when we repeat the same thought or behavior, the brain physically strengthens the neural pathways associated with it. The more often we repeat a thought, the more natural it feels. As Dr. Kendra Cherry explains in her article "What is

Memory Consolidation?", "the more frequently signals are passed, the stronger the synapses become." The brain literally learns what we practice.[2]

That means if your internal script has been, *I can't,* for years, it will feel true, even if it isn't. By interrupting that thought, even once, you are beginning to carve out a new path. With every repetition, that new path grows stronger.

The cost of not interrupting the script is high. Left alone, the old voice keeps reinforcing itself. It whispers, *See? You stayed quiet again. You really don't have anything to add.* That's how silence becomes identity. But the truth is, silence is not who you are. It's only a habit.

And habits can change.

~~~~~

---

[2]Cherry, Kendra. "What is Memory Consolidation?" Verywell Mind (2024). https://www.verywellmind.com/what-is-memory-consolidation-2795355?utm

Writing a New Script

Interrupting the old voice is one thing. But the real transformation happens when you begin to write a new script. One that aligns with who you truly want to become.

After I made the decision to no longer live under the weight of my negative inner voice, something powerful happened. I discovered that I actually loved speaking. Not just talking for the sake of filling space, but speaking with intention, especially to empowered audiences. Every time I shared in a meeting, it brought something alive in me — a leadership side that wanted to do more, to lead more, to step into responsibility. Speaking revealed a new version of myself that was confident, capable, and ready to grow.

That shift didn't happen overnight. Shortly after making that decision, I went through one of the roughest patches of my life. I left the role I was in and spent months unemployed, alone, and questioning what was next. And yet, it was during that quiet season that I leaned on my new inner script the most. Every day, I stood in front of the mirror, looked into my own eyes, and spoke life into myself:

★ You are strong.
★ You are capable.
★ You are a leader.

Over and over, I affirmed the truth: I was choosing to believe.

Then one day, I saw a posting for a compliance manager position. I had never managed anyone in my life. By all logic, I was not "qualified." But my new script reminded me that I didn't need to be perfect... I just needed to show up.

I applied. The night before the interview, I paced my living room, practicing out loud the same affirmations I had repeated for months. I rehearsed my answers, but more importantly, I reminded myself that confidence matters as much as credentials. I interviewed. I spoke from the confidence and the strength I had been rehearsing in private — and I got the role.

I will never forget the hiring manager asking me how much I wanted to be paid. I stated my range and the value I knew I could deliver. She nodded, countered within the range, and we aligned before I left the building. That moment seared itself into my memory because it was proof that my words, the ones that I had spoken to myself in the mirror for months, were now shaping my reality. The fear that had once kept me silent was still there, but it no longer controlled me. What I had practiced in private had carried me through one of the biggest leaps of my career.

My new inner dialogue was no longer just practice. It had become my voice, my confidence, and my calling.

The very first place to begin is with yourself. Too often, we wait for encouragement from others — a mentor, colleague, a friend — and while those voices can help, they can never replace your own. One of the most damaging beliefs is that the best advice or encouragement must come from outside of you. That's simply not true. The most powerful source of change will always be your own inner dialogue.

Start by paying attention to what your inner voice is saying. Notice the words that echo in your head right before you speak, the phrases that rise up when you feel nervous or doubtful. Maybe it tells you, *You can't do this. You're not good enough. Everyone will notice if you fail.* Those phrases feel automatic, but they're not the truth. They're the remnants of old experiences, old fears, old scripts you've carried for too long. Recognizing them is the first step. As Shakespeare wrote in Hamlet, "to thine own self be true." You can't shift your inner voice until you know what it's really saying to you. Only then can you begin to rewrite it with honesty and purpose.

Once you have named it, you can begin to create a new script. That doesn't mean pretending the negative voice is gone. It means teaching your inner dialogue something new. When you catch yourself rehearsing failure, stop and replace it with a truth you choose to believe. Fill that inner space with new words, new memories, and new affirmations that reflect who you are becoming.

It won't happen all at once. There will still be moments when the old voice whispers, *This is silly. Stay quiet. Don't push yourself.* You may even listen sometimes. But over time, as you practice speaking positively to yourself, the balance shifts. The positive grows stronger, the negative weakens, and eventually the new scripts become your default.

And here's something to remember: self-doubt isn't always the enemy. In small doses, it can actually push you to grow, to reach deeper, and to rise higher. Doubt can push us to dig deeper, to pull from the core of who we are, and to rise up with greater boldness. In fact, many people have achieved incredible success because they faced voices of doubt (internal or external) that they chose to rise above. That doubt sparked a fire, a drive to prove themselves capable of more.

Imagine being in a classroom or a meeting where someone is speaking, but the room is so noisy you can barely hear them. That is what happens with your inner voice. It's speaking, but the noise of self-doubt, fear, and outside pressure often drowns it out. To hear it clearly, you need moments to be quiet.

That quiet might look like time alone in your room, a walk in the park, or even a short getaway. It's about tuning out the noise of everyday life so you can listen to what your inner voice is really saying. Scripture illustrates this pattern through Christ, who often withdrew from the crowds and even from his disciples to spend time in prayer and communion with God. To receive direction, he stepped away from the noise. In the same way, we too need moments of stillness to reflect, to pray, and to reconnect with our inner truth.

In that quiet space, you can begin to uncover the roots of your patterns. What drives you to speak? What stops you from speaking? What memories resurface when it's your turn to share? These questions open the door to healing.

If you struggle with self-doubt or negative self-talk, remember this: you are not alone. Most of us, at some point in life, have battled the quiet voice that says, *You're not enough.* The difference is whether you choose to tune out the noise and put life-giving words into yourself. Take a moment to stand in front of a mirror. Look directly into your own eyes. Scripture tells us that "the eye is the lamp of the body" (Matthew 6:22 NIV), and in that moment, you are looking into the place where your inner voice resides. Begin to speak life into your soul. Tell yourself the truth that God already sees: You are chosen. You are enough. You are growing.

At the end of the day, no one can speak for you. Yes, God is your ultimate guide, but after Him, it's you. You are your biggest advocate. If you're struggling to speak up, pause and ask yourself: who is going to do it for me? The answer is simple: no one can do it better, and no one was meant to. No one can truly represent your truth, your purpose, or your voice; only *you* can.

Part of growing up is taking responsibility for your own voice. Owning it. Choosing to speak so that your perspective, your wisdom, and your truth are heard. This isn't just a personal matter; it's also a contribution to the world around you. A healthy community, whether at work, in church, or in society at large, depends on the voices of its members.

Too often, we step back and let a small group of people lead, decide, and shape outcomes. And then we complain about the results. But what if we had spoken up earlier? What if our voices had been part of the conversation? The outcome could have been different, sometimes drastically so.

Speaking up is more than a skill; it is a responsibility. Your voice matters not just for your growth, but for the growth of those around you. If you don't bring it to the table, the world is left missing something only you can contribute.

Reflection: Meeting Your Inner Voice

Take a moment to sit quietly and simply notice your inner voice. What is it saying right now? Is it encouraging, critical, fearful, or dismissive? Pay attention to the thoughts that arise when you are about to speak or take action. Do not judge yourself for what you hear; just observe it. As you do this, begin to notice patterns. Are there recurring phrases you tell yourself? Are certain situations triggering a louder, more critical voice?

Next, connect these observations to your purpose. Reflect on how these thoughts influence your actions or decisions. If you were to rewrite them to support your goals, what would they say? Choose one recurring negative thought and create a positive, empowering alternative. Say it out loud. Look at yourself in a mirror if you can, and repeat it daily. Notice even the small shifts in confidence, tone, or willingness to speak up.

Finally, take a few minutes to journal. Ask yourself: What does my inner voice want to believe today? What is it holding me back from? What would I tell a friend in this exact situation? Awareness is the first step. You don't need to silence the old voice overnight. You only need to notice it and begin to write a new script that empowers you, moves you forward, and helps you speak your truth.

As you move forward, remember that this is a practice, not a one-time task. Each conversation, each pause, and each moment of awareness is an opportunity to rewrite your story. You are training your voice, building courage, and claiming your place in the world. Start small. Speak kindly to yourself, and recognize the power you hold when you choose to override doubt with purpose.

In the next chapter, we'll explore how to take that awareness and turn it into confidence, step by step, so your voice can be heard loud, clear, and fully yours.

CHAPTER 4

Building Confidence And Projection

Up until now, we have explored the inner landscape of your voice. The doubts, the fears, and the silent moments that have shaped you. Awareness is essential, but awareness alone does not create change. Confidence begins inside, yet it becomes visible only when you step forward.

Turning awareness into action means moving from reflection to practice. It is about testing your voice, experimenting with your words, and daring to be seen even when your heart races or your hands shake. Confidence is not the absence of fear; it is the decision to act in spite of it. Every time you choose to speak, to contribute, or to take a small risk, you are bridging the gap between who you are privately and who you show up as publicly.

In my mid-twenties, while working at my company, I began to realize how essential it was for me to find and use my voice. The emotions were intense: frustration because I felt like I had to reshape my Jamaican accent, frustration at trying to speak "properly" in a world that demanded perfect grammar. I questioned whether I belonged, wondering if I was really cut out for this space.

Alongside frustration came sadness and self-pity. I felt I should have already mastered these skills by age twenty-four or twenty-five. Where I was, some people already questioned my ability, but staying in that role felt safer than leaving. I feared that stepping into a new opportunity might expose me even more, that a new manager would doubt my competence or dismiss me as a fraud. Concern and self-doubt became constant companions.

Yet I knew I had to act. The turning point came when I signed up for the Dale Carnegie course — a leap that changed everything. My company approved the training, and I realized that taking the risk now, facing fear and potential failure, was far better than staying silent in a false sense of security. Confidence began with a single decision to try, and over time, it became visible in how I spoke, interacted, and showed up in the world.

That moment taught me that authentic confidence is not flawless speech or effortless boldness. It is choosing to step forward even when fear, doubt, or self-pity want to hold you back. It is action rooted in purpose, self-awareness, and courage.

This chapter will guide you through taking those first steps. From speaking up in meetings to initiating conversations and volunteering ideas. You will learn that confidence is built moment by moment. It grows through action, practice, and permission to fail, learn, and try again.

Now is the time to move from thought to action. The inner work is done; the stage is yours.

⌒‿⌒

Redefining Confidence

True confidence is not the absence of weakness; it is the strength to stand firm even when you feel uncertain. It is recognizing that fear, doubt, or imperfection do not disqualify you from stepping forward. Even the greatest speakers continue to train, to practice, to strengthen their skills. We may feel confident on stage, but once the spotlight is gone, we must keep building and growing that confidence, just like exercising a muscle.

Confidence, for me, is giving every speaking opportunity a chance. It means speaking even when my voice trembles, when others seem stronger, or when I fear I might not be heard. It means sharing my thoughts and ideas, knowing there will be mistakes or misunderstandings. I may stumble over my grammar or encounter someone who does not want to hear me speak, but I still choose to use my voice. Confidence means not allowing anyone, others, circumstances, or even my own inner doubts to deter me from contributing my voice to society and to the groups I am part of.

Sometimes, confidence means standing alone. It means becoming your own supporter, your own cheerleader. It means believing in yourself even when the odds feel against you. And when things go wrong, confidence is not about pretending they didn't. Even when a speech falls short or a moment fails to meet expectations, confidence is the resolve to come back, to try again, and to grow from the experience.

Faith and understanding form the deepest foundation of this confidence. Over time, I began to see a pattern: every time I spoke, no matter how afraid I felt, something good followed. My words connected with someone or encouraged a listener. This awareness allowed me to stand firmly when I spoke. I now recognize that what God has placed in us is greater than anything outside of us. This awareness allows us to stand firmly when we speak. God has placed us here for a purpose — to make a meaningful impact in someone's life, to contribute to your team, or to inspire others in ways you may never fully see. Confidence grounded in faith allows me to speak, even when I cannot predict the effect of my words.

I think of Jeremiah in the Bible. When God called him to speak to the nations, Jeremiah hesitated, saying, "I do not know how to speak; I am too young." But God reminded him, "Do not be afraid, for I am with you" (Jeremiah 1:6–8 KJV). Like Jeremiah, we often doubt our readiness or our ability, forgetting that when God calls us to speak, He also equips us. Real confidence begins when we trust that truth. Trust that God is with us, even when we stumble, falter, or speak imperfectly. Where we are weak, strength can manifest through others or through divine guidance. When we are alone, God can be our mouthpiece.

Confidence goes beyond courage or technical skill. It is the full understanding that you do not speak alone; God's presence accompanies every word. It is faith in motion. He is with us when we stutter, when we stumble, when our words falter. Faith transforms our fear into courage, our hesitation into action, and our weakness into a channel for purpose. This is what confidence means to me today, as it relates to speaking, leading, and showing up in the world.

_____

Real Confidence vs. Fake Confidence

Confidence doesn't always look the same. Sometimes what appears strong on the outside is built on uncertainty within. Many people look confident because they have learned how to hide doubt well, but authentic confidence is something much deeper. It is steady, not because it knows everything, but because it stands on preparation, truth, and faith.

I remember one moment that revealed this difference to me clearly. I was working in internal audit when my manager asked if I understood the laws of New York State related to Anti-Money Laundering (AML) compliance. I understood them only at a basic level, but I squared my shoulders and answered as if I did. My response happened to be correct, but deep down, I knew I was guessing. That was not real confidence... It was what I now call in-between confidence. It looked steady on the outside, but underneath, it lacked foundation.

That moment taught me something valuable. There are times when we "fake it until we make it." Every speaker knows the feeling of stepping onto a stage with nerves and finding that confidence arrives only once after they begin. In those moments, "fake" confidence can be a bridge that helps you start, but it cannot be a home where you stay.

Fake confidence is fragile. It comes from pride, from rushing to answer without preparation, or from performing superiority to hide insecurity. It thrives on comparison, feeding on the illusion of being "better" than others. It often masks fear rather than addressing it. And while it may work for a moment, it eventually collapses because it is not rooted in truth.

Real confidence is different. It does not pretend to know everything. It is built on humility, preparation, and self-awareness. It allows you to admit when you need help, to pause before answering, and to listen rather than dominate. It is not loud or showy; it is steady. It doesn't come from proving yourself to others but from aligning with your own values and preparation.

The difference between the two may seem small, but it changes everything.

- ★ Fake confidence seeks to impress. Real confidence seeks to connect.
- ★ Fake confidence is about control. Real confidence is about presence.
- ★ Fake confidence performs. Real confidence is built on preparation.

You do not have to choose perfectly between the two. Sometimes fake confidence is a stepping stone, giving you just enough courage to start. But over time, as you grow, the goal is to cultivate authenticity, to let your inner certainty and ongoing growth show up in the way you speak, lead, and live. Because while fake confidence may carry you for a moment, authentic confidence will carry you forward.

I once worked for a manager who made me question my worth. Every day, I showed up ready to prove myself, arriving early, staying late, and checking every detail of my reports. When she brought in a reviewer to evaluate my work, I felt nervous but hopeful. A few days later, he told her that my report was strong, detailed, and impressive. For a moment, I thought my effort had finally been recognized.

What I didn't know was that behind my back, my manager had told the reviewer not to share that feedback with me. She wanted to take the credit and make it look as if my work was hers. When I found out, it felt like the ground had dropped beneath me. It wasn't just professional disappointment; it was personal. I felt invisible. Small. Like all the care and integrity I had poured into my work suddenly meant nothing.

That night, I sat with my phone in my hand, staring at the screen. I sent a message to the man I was dating, telling him how discouraged I felt, how ready I was to give up. He called me right away. I still remember his voice, calm but firm, telling me to lift my head. He reminded me of who I was, of how every hardship I had faced had only made me stronger. He said that pressure does not destroy diamonds; it creates them. His words reached places I did not even realize were still hurting.

For the first time in weeks, I felt my strength return. Not because I forced confidence, but because someone helped me remember the truth that was already mine.

Being impressive focuses on how others see you. It is about performance, perfection, and control. But being impactful is about how others feel after hearing you. It goes beyond appearance.

That is the true shift—from acting confident to becoming confident. It is something you build from within preparation, truth, and connection. When you speak or lead from that place, people don't just listen—they connect.

Mentality and Projection

I think confidence is not simply what comes out of your mouth or the actions you take. It begins in your mind. How you think about yourself before speaking, how you prepare, and how you project your energy all shape how others experience you. Developing a strong mentality is not just about rehearsing what to say but cultivating a belief system that supports your voice. When you believe that your words carry purpose, that belief translates into tone, presence, and energy.

Preparation is key. Start with research. Understand the topic, anticipate questions, and gather the facts you need to feel grounded. Knowledge builds the foundation for confidence, and when you know your material, hesitation and self-doubt have less room to creep in.

Then, practice. Speak aloud in front of a mirror. Notice your posture, gestures, and tone. Watch how your energy shifts when you adjust your stance, make eye contact, or emphasize key words. The mirror is more than a reflection of your face. It's a reflection of your presence. Practicing this way trains both mind and body to communicate from a place of truth, not just words.

Projection goes beyond speaking loudly. It goes beyond volume. It is the act of sending your energy and intention out into the room so that your audience not only hears your words, but *feels* them. Projection includes your tone, pace, eye contact, gestures, and even subtle expression. It's about showing up fully, so your message lands with clarity and confidence. Projection communicates authenticity: when you speak from your knowledge and conviction, your audience senses that what you are saying matters, and so it does.

Feedback matters. I share my practice with trusted friends or mentors and ask them to notice not just my words, but my energy, clarity, and presence. Ask them to observe not just your words, but your energy, clarity, and presence. Honest feedback helps you refine your delivery while staying true to yourself.

It also teaches you that projection is a skill that can be strengthened with guidance and reflection.

Recording yourself can be a game-changer. Sometimes, I listen back and am proud of how clearly I spoke and how confidently my ideas came through. The more I listen to myself, the more I want to speak. Each playback reminds me that my voice matters, that I have something valuable to contribute, and that I can make an impact simply by showing up and saying what I mean. It feels empowering in ways I didn't speak. It feels good to recognize my voice, to realize I can command attention, persuade, and advocate for myself. It teaches me where I stumble, yes, but also where I shine. It reminds me that the voice I carry is capable, that I am capable, and that I deserve to be heard. Each time I hit "record," I'm practicing not just my words, but my courage and my ability to step fully into the space I occupy.

Projection also means self-advocacy. I remember a manager once saying I was not a good note-taker. I set my pen down, took a deep breath, and calmly said, "I don't believe that's true," then explained my reasoning. Another time, a manager was rude and persistent in questioning me. I repeated my answer, clearly and calmly, defending my point without losing my composure. These moments taught me that my voice is my own advocate, my defender. Using it with clarity and confidence creates space for respect, for understanding, and for action.

Ultimately, mentality and projection form a bridge between who you are inside and how you show up outside. It is about aligning confidence, knowledge, and authenticity so that your voice carries beyond words. It carries energy, conviction, and impact. When your mind is grounded, your preparation thorough, and your practice intentional, your voice carries beyond words. It carries confidence, authenticity, and impact.

And finally, remember that projection is not just about your strength: it's also about trust. Before you speak, take a moment to pray, breathe, or ground yourself in faith. Believe that God has given you a voice worth hearing and that you don't stand alone when you step forward. When your heart is rooted in faith, your projection carries not only confidence but peace. And when I speak, it is not just words. It is presence, purpose, and power.

Reflection: Presence Over Performance

Your mentality shapes your message long before a single word leaves your mouth. Our inner dialogue is already deciding how the world will receive you. If your thoughts are filled with doubt, fear, or the urge to impress, those feelings will leak through no matter how polished your words are. But if your thoughts are rooted in truth, preparation, and faith, then your message carries a weight that others can feel.

Projection is the outward expression of that inner reality. To project is not simply to speak louder, but to let your conviction reach the room. It is to believe so deeply in what you're saying that your voice, body, and presence all work together to deliver it. When you project from a place of authenticity, you stop performing and start connecting. And connection is where transformation happens. For you, and for the people listening.

So the next time you prepare to speak, do not focus only on your slides or notes. Ask yourself: What is my mentality going in? Am I grounded in truth, or am I trying to perform? Am I projecting presence, or am I hiding behind words?

This week, choose one moment to practice. It doesn't have to be a stage; it could be a conversation with your boss, a presentation in class, or even sharing your thoughts at a family dinner. Before you speak, pause. Breathe. Ground yourself in what you know and who you are. Then, project, not to impress, but to connect.

Because the world doesn't just need more voices. It needs voices that carry strength, clarity, and faith. And that begins with you.

CHAPTER 5

Starting Small, Stepping Up

I still remember the day I decided to raise my hand in a small meeting. It wasn't a stage. There were no bright lights. Just a regular conference room, a few coworkers, and a conversation I usually stayed silent in. But something in me shifted that day. My heart was racing, my palms were damp, and my mind was filled with a thousand reasons to stay quiet. But before I could talk myself out of it, I heard my own voice say, "I have a thought."

It wasn't perfect. My words stumbled a little. My accent came through strongly. But the moment I finished, something powerful happened: people turned their heads. They listened. That single moment reminded me of something far bigger than the room I was in.

It reminded me of Tammy. Tammy was a little girl who stuttered so severely that speaking in class terrified her. One day, her teacher, Cynthia, noticed that Tammy fainted just before giving a class speech. Instead of letting the moment pass, Cynthia made a decision. She took Tammy under her wing, determined to help her find her voice. She encouraged Tammy to join the class speaking competition. Tammy agreed, but her first attempt was a disaster. She stumbled through the speech, froze midway, and walked off the stage in tears. She wanted to quit.

That's when Cynthia shared her own story. As a child, she, too, had been ridiculed and laughed at when she tried to speak. Someone had believed in her then; someone had helped her find her voice. Now, she wanted to do the same for Tammy. She told her, "If I can do it, so can you. Your voice is inside you. You just have to release it."

With Cynthia's mentorship, Tammy kept practicing, little by little. She spoke in front of two classmates, then five, then the whole class again. It took years of patience, practice, and small steps. But by her final year of high school, Tammy entered another speaking competition. This time, she didn't faint. She didn't freeze. She spoke with clarity, strength, and presence. And years later, Tammy became one of the world's most celebrated public speakers.

Her story shows something simple but profound: greatness doesn't begin on the big stage. It begins in the small spaces, the quiet classrooms, the moments when no one is cheering. It grows through practice, patience, and the willingness to keep trying after failure.

For me, that meeting was my version of Tammy's classroom. It was my training ground. It was the first moment I gave myself permission to step forward, even in a small space. What surprised me most was how much power lives inside small beginnings. Speaking up in a small room that day didn't just change that meeting. It started to change me.

Small settings don't feel glamorous. They don't come with applause or spotlights. But they are where courage is built. They are where shaky voices grow steadier, where hesitant hands learn to rise without overthinking. They are where confidence starts to take root.

Before you can confidently speak to a room full of people, lead a meeting, or present in front of a high-stakes audience, you need to start small. Small moments matter often more than we realize. Every time you speak in a one-on-one conversation, a small group, or even in a casual setting, you are practicing the muscles of your voice, your presence, and your confidence.

These small moments are where the groundwork is laid. They are where you experiment, where you stumble, where you discover what your voice can truly do, and more importantly, where you start to believe that your voice deserves to be heard.

I know how tempting it is to focus on the big moments: the promotions, the presentations, the speeches that feel like life-or-death tests of your ability. I've been there. I've wanted to impress, to prove that I belonged, and sometimes that desire made me rush, speak too fast, or overcompensate with words that weren't really mine. I've tried to sound smarter than I was, use words I didn't fully understand, and perform for others instead of showing up authentically. And every time I did that, I stumbled. The words didn't flow. My energy felt off. I realized quickly that trying to impress others often does more harm than good. True confidence doesn't come from looking good to others: it comes from showing up as yourself and trusting your own voice.

That's why starting small is so important. In a smaller setting, you can speak without the weight of expectation. You can make mistakes, learn from them, and notice how your words land without fear of judgment. You can explore your tone, your pacing, your gestures, and how your presence fills the space. Every time you speak in these low-pressure moments, you are strengthening your voice, your confidence, and your ability to connect. Every small win is building a foundation that will carry you when the stakes are higher.

I remember one of my first intentions: small wins. I started practicing in front of a mirror, recording my voice, and listening to it over and over. I realized that I had been speaking too softly, too quickly, too unsure of myself. I didn't project my energy in a way that matched my personality. It felt strange at first, almost uncomfortable, to hear my own voice booming back at me from the recorder. But little by little, I adjusted. I practiced projecting, pausing, and emphasizing the words that mattered the most. I noticed how my energy shifted when my mind aligned with my voice.

Starting small also teaches you how to manage your nerves. There is something about a smaller audience, a familiar group, or even just a one-on-one conversation that allows you to feel the tension in your body, recognize it, and work with it. You learn that taking deep breaths, grounding yourself, and centering your mind before you speak makes a difference, whether you are talking to a friend, a coworker, or eventually, a crowd.

In this chapter, we will explore how to step into a smaller setting first. We will look at the importance of practicing intentionally, of reflecting on what works and what doesn't, and of using each small interaction as a building block for larger success. You will learn how to approach these moments with purpose, how to take note of the small wins, and how to gradually expand your comfort zone. By the time you step into a bigger room, a presentation, or a critical conversation, you'll already have a track record of small wins that give you real, grounded confidence.

Starting small is not a shortcut; it is the essential work that ensures you are ready for the larger stages in life. It is where your confidence grows quietly, incrementally, and sustainably. It is where your voice becomes strong, not because you are trying to impress anyone, but because you are discovering the strength that already lives inside you. And once you recognize that strength, the bigger stages won't feel intimidating; they will feel like another opportunity to show up fully, with clarity, purpose, and impact.

So let's begin here, in the small moments. Let's step up, one conversation, one meeting, one interaction at a time. Because it is in these small moments that your voice finds its power, your confidence grows its roots, and your courage prepares for the world to hear you.

The Power of Small Settings

When I look back at my own journey, I realize that the most powerful shifts didn't happen on a stage in front of hundreds of people. They happened in the small, almost hidden spaces of my life. A casual conversation in the hallway. Speaking up in a team meeting. Answering a question in class when my heart was pounding. These moments may have seemed small on the surface, but they became my training ground.

That is the power of small settings: they give us room to grow without the crushing weight of perfection. They are forgiving. They are flexible. They allow us to stumble, recover, and try again. When you start small, you learn that mistakes are not the end of the world. They are simply part of the practice.

I remember the first time I dared to raise my hand in a group setting. It wasn't a speech, it wasn't a presentation: it was just one sentence. I felt my throat tighten as I spoke, but when I saw heads nodding and someone even smiling in agreement, I realized something: my words had landed. It didn't matter that it was just one comment. It mattered that I had shown up.

Small settings are powerful because they emphasize relationships over performance. In a big speech, it can feel like all eyes are on you, waiting to be impressed. But in smaller spaces, the focus shifts. It becomes less about proving yourself and more about connecting with the people in front of you. You notice their reactions. You respond to their energy. And in that exchange, something authentic is built.

When I stopped thinking of small settings as "less important" and began treating them as opportunities, everything changed. A one-on-one conversation with a colleague became a chance to practice clarity. A coffee chat with a mentor turned into a lesson in storytelling. Even ordering food at a restaurant became a practice in projecting my voice and speaking with confidence. These were not just errands or passing interactions. They were micro-stages, and I was rehearsing every single time.

There are so many everyday spaces where speaking opportunities quietly exist, but we overlook them because they don't look like "public speaking." Think about a small prayer group at church, where you could share a short reflection or lead a prayer. Consider the local community center, where stepping up to welcome people or help coordinate a meeting is a chance to practice presence. Volunteering at work, even just to give a quick update during a team call, is another training space. Leading a parent-teacher meeting or simply speaking up respectfully to advocate for your child also builds muscle.

And perhaps the most overlooked of all: speaking up for yourself in everyday situations, whether that's clarifying something with a manager, asking a question at a store, or voicing your opinion in a conversation. These are small moments, but they count.

The more you practice in these small, everyday spaces, the more natural it feels when you step into bigger ones. You've already built the muscle of speaking up, of recovering from a stumble, of leaning into connection. You've already proven to yourself that your voice carries weight, even if it's only one sentence at a time.

Think about it: every small setting is a micro-moment of courage. Raising your hand in class. Offering an idea in a meeting. Sharing your perspective in a group discussion. These are not insignificant acts. They are bricks, each one laid down as you build the foundation of your confidence. Over time, those bricks stack into something strong enough to support you on any stage.

Think about your own experiences. Can you recall a moment when a simple conversation changed how you saw yourself, encouraged you to act, or opened a new opportunity? Small exchanges often hold big lessons.

There's also something powerful about small settings. They remind us that communication is not just about performance; it is about presence. People may not remember every word you say, but they will remember how you made them feel in those moments. And small spaces give us the freedom to focus less on being polished and more on being real. That authenticity is what lingers.

So, let me ask you this: Where are the small stages in your daily life that you might be overlooking? Maybe it's speaking up during your next team meeting instead of staying silent. Maybe it's sharing an idea with a friend, even if you're unsure how it will land. Maybe it's practicing your storytelling at dinner with family. These are the places where your confidence quietly takes root.

I encourage you not to dismiss them. Don't tell yourself, *This is too small to matter.* Every stage matters. Every time you open your mouth, you are shaping not only how others perceive you, but how you perceive yourself. Confidence is not built in leaps. It is built in layers. And the smallest settings often hold the greatest power to transform us from the inside out.

The big stage will come in time. But your preparation for it begins now. In the small, everyday moments where you dare to use your voice. Embrace them. Practice with them. Learn from them. Because one day, when you stand in front of a larger crowd, you will realize something incredible: you have already been training for this all along.

~~~~~~

Small Steps, Big Shifts

When I look back, many of my biggest leaps began with small, almost ordinary actions. They didn't happen on a stage or behind a podium. They happened in quiet corners of meetings, casual conversations, and everyday moments that I might have overlooked if I hadn't made a conscious choice to step forward.

In the beginning, I focused on micro-moments. For example, I would volunteer to introduce someone new in a meeting. It wasn't a long or elaborate speech — just a short introduction — but each time I did it, it chipped away at the fear that kept me silent. I also started summarizing discussions when meetings were ending. Saying something like, "So just to recap what we agreed on..." gave me a natural opening to speak without the pressure of having to come up with something groundbreaking.

Another thing I practiced was asking one clear, thoughtful question. Whether in a work setting, a training session, or a casual group, asking a question helped me insert my voice in a structured way. Over time, this became a habit. I didn't have to be the loudest person in the room. I just needed to keep showing up in these small ways.

Small settings are powerful because they give you space to learn without the heavy weight of perfection. If you stumble, you recover quickly. If you forget a word, no one writes it down as evidence against you. These moments are where you train your voice, test your presence, and build the mental muscle to keep speaking.

It's easy to dream of the big stage: the spotlight, the applause, the moment everyone listens. You want to give the keynote, lead the presentation, or speak in front of hundreds without going through the "smaller" steps. I get it. But every speaker you admire started somewhere small. Oprah Winfrey once practiced in local studios before her voice reached the world.[3] Martin

Luther King Jr. preached to small congregations before he inspired a movement.[4]

The small settings are the training ground that makes the big stages possible. You cannot build endurance by sprinting your first mile. Confidence grows through repetition in safe spaces. Every time you speak in a small setting, you're not wasting time — you're laying bricks for the foundation that will hold you up when the crowd gets bigger and the pressure higher. Each small space prepares you for the next.

And to those who feel embarrassed, like speaking in front of two or three people "doesn't count" — it absolutely does. Speaking in small groups is not less; it's smart. The small spaces give you the freedom to experiment, make mistakes, and find your rhythm. Some of my most important growth didn't come from standing on a stage. It came from these intimate settings where my voice had room to breathe. If you can learn to hold the attention of three people with authenticity and clarity, you can grow that skill to thirty, three hundred, or more.

And here's the thing: your first audience doesn't have to be people. It can be your pets, a mirror, or even an empty room. For me, during my previous marriage, we had fish in the living room, and I often practiced by talking to them. That was my audience. So if you find yourself practicing in front of your pets or in an empty room, don't feel bad about that. Small beginnings lead to big things.

There is something beautiful about starting small. When you speak to two or three people, you don't face a sea of eyes. You can focus on one or two friendly faces. In fact, there's a technique I still use: when you're speaking to a crowd, find one friendly face in the audience and return to that face whenever you feel nervous. It grounds you. Starting small trains you to manage those moments. Just like lifting weights, you don't start with the heaviest barbell. You begin with one pound, then two, then five. Over time, your strength grows.

Starting small also makes your story sweeter. It gives you experience that your audience can relate to because most of us begin in the same way. We all have those moments of talking to pets, mirrors, or two trusted friends. And when you share your journey, people see themselves in your story.

I think of this through a story that still guides me today. Years ago, I had a set of flowers that simply refused to grow. I watered them, I cared for them, and still they remained the same size. One day, just for decoration, I bought new pots that were much larger than the ones I had. I moved the flowers into the bigger pots, and not long after, something remarkable happened: the flowers grew to fill the space. I didn't expect it, but they were ready. They had been ready all along; they just needed room.

That moment taught me that we are often more prepared than we think. Growth doesn't always happen because we feel fully ready. Sometimes, it happens because we give ourselves space to grow. I've experienced this in my own career. Once, I was placed on an internal audit where the client spoke Mandarin. I didn't speak Mandarin, and at first glance, it looked like I wasn't ready for the assignment. But I leaned in, did my research, and found ways to understand enough to complete the work. I grew into that space through practice and persistence. That experience showed me that even when the task feels beyond me, I can grow to meet it.

The same is true when it comes to speaking. You may not feel fully ready to step onto a larger stage, but readiness isn't always something you have beforehand. Often, it develops as you go. Les Brown tells a story about how his high school teacher pushed him to speak in front of the class. The first time, he trembled and stepped back down. But he didn't stop there. He returned, and with each try, he grew more confident until he ruled that stage. Growth happens in motion, not in waiting for the "perfect" moment.

I once heard it said that the inner self has to meet the outer world through practice. I believe that. Inside each of us is the ability to rise to new spaces, but we have to allow ourselves to be stretched. Like the flowers in the new pot, we grow to meet the space we step into. That doesn't mean we should neglect preparation. If you're giving a speech on a technical topic, you need to study and equip yourself. But don't mistake imperfection for unreadiness. You may not feel flawless, but that doesn't mean you're unqualified.

I think of a young preacher I once knew. He had a fire in his heart to become a great minister. But his pastor didn't rush him to the podium. He had him sit at the front, observe, serve, and grow. He watched him lead at home, take on responsibilities in the church, and immerse himself in the Word. Years later, when the time came, that young preacher stepped up and spoke with power and clarity. His preparation happened over time, quietly, through the everyday moments of growth.

That's exactly how small speaking opportunities work. They shape you for bigger spaces. You may not think you're ready for that next level, but as you practice, reflect, and stretch yourself, you grow into it — just like those flowers filling a larger pot. When the moment comes, you'll find that the strength is already within you. All it needed was space to flourish.

So I want you to think about your own life. Where are the small stages you've been overlooking? It might be a team huddle, a group chat, a classroom discussion, a church meeting, or even a family dinner. These are the places where you can start showing up consistently, without pressure, without waiting for a "perfect" moment.

This week, choose one or two small spaces and set a clear intention: raise your hand once, offer a thought, summarize a conversation, or introduce someone. It doesn't have to be big. It just has to be intentional. Over time, these moments create momentum. They turn hesitation into habit and habit into confidence.

The big stages will come. But first, honor the small ones. That's where your voice is forged.

$\smile$

[3] Winfrey, Oprah. Academy of Achievement. Available at:
https://achievement.org/achiever/oprah-winfrey
[4] King, Jr. Martin Luther. "Sermons and Speeches of Martin Luther King Jr." Wikipedia. Available at:
https://en.wikipedia.org/wiki/Sermons_and_speeches_of_Martin_Luther_King_Jr.

Reflection: Honoring the Small Stage

I want you to pause and reflect on your own journey. Think about the places you move through each day: your workplace, classrooms, family gatherings, community groups, even casual conversations with friends. How many of these moments offer small but real opportunities to speak, and how many of them pass unnoticed because they seem too insignificant?

Small settings are often overlooked, but they give you something precious. They allow room to breathe and space to grow. In these environments, you can try things out, stumble, learn, and recover without the weight of high expectations. A smaller audience is usually more forgiving, and these moments often carry less pressure, which makes them perfect for practice.

Take a moment to ask yourself a few honest questions:

★ Where are the small spaces in my daily life that I have not used to speak up?
★ When was the last time I made a conscious decision to speak up in one of those moments?
★ How might my voice grow if I treated these moments as valuable training grounds rather than unimportant occasions?

Now it is time to take action. Over the next week, choose at least two small settings where you will intentionally speak up. These moments do not need to be elaborate. It might be introducing someone in a team meeting, summarizing a discussion in a group, asking a thoughtful question in class, or sharing a brief insight with a friend. The goal is not perfection. It is to practice showing up.

Before you speak, take a deep breath. Remind yourself that this is practice, not performance. Speak clearly and allow your voice to carry. Focus on connection rather than impressing anyone. Afterward, take a few minutes to reflect on how it went. You can write your thoughts down or simply sit with the memory. Ask yourself: What worked well? How did it feel to use my voice at that moment? What surprised me? What would I try differently next time?

These reflections will help you notice patterns in your growth. Over time, you will begin to recognize the moments when hesitation arises and the moments when your voice feels stronger than you expected. Each of these experiences adds to your foundation.

Remember, there is no stage too small when it comes to building confidence. These spaces are not warm-ups for something greater. They are the real work of finding and strengthening your voice. When you honor the small stage, you prepare yourself for the larger ones that will come later.

Part Three

Putting It in Practice

CHAPTER 6

Managing Nerves And Structuring Your Message

There are moments in life that make your heart race before you even begin to speak. Speaking in front of others is one of those moments. I know what it feels like to want to hide, to hope someone else will speak on your behalf, to feel like your voice is too small for the task in front of you.

I wish I could tell you that nerves disappear once you become more experienced, but the truth is, they never really leave. I still feel my palms sweat. My voice still shakes sometimes. My heart still pounds before I open my mouth to speak. The difference now is not that I am free of nerves, but that I have learned how to walk with them, manage them, and even use them as energy.

For a long time, I thought being nervous meant I was not good enough. If I was meant to be a speaker, I imagined my body would be calm, my hands steady, my voice smooth. But nerves are not proof of weakness. They are proof that you care. They are your body's way of preparing you for something that matters. What makes the difference is how you channel that energy.

I remember sitting outside a meeting room early in my career, notes trembling in my hand. I had worked hard to prepare, but as soon as I heard my name called, fear rushed through me like a wave. My throat tightened, my legs felt heavy, and all I could think was, *What if I forget everything?*

In that moment, it wasn't the lack of preparation that almost silenced me; it was the belief that nerves meant I could not do it.

I also had to learn that nerves are not my enemy. They are simply energy. And that energy can be directed. Instead of letting it spiral into self-doubt, I learned to channel it into focus. Before important conversations or meetings, I prepare carefully. I do my research so I feel grounded in what I'm about to say. I think through my key points and how I want to say them. Sometimes, I even practice in front of the mirror or record myself, not to memorize a script, but to hear how my voice sounds and to get comfortable with the rhythm of my speech.

Managing nerves is not about eliminating fear; it's about creating a foundation that allows you to speak through it. Faith gives me peace. Preparation gives me grounding. Structure gives me a sense of direction. And experience teaches me that each time I step forward, the nerves lose a little more power.

This chapter is about exactly that: learning to manage the nerves that rise before you speak and structuring your message so your words come through with strength and clarity. Whether you're addressing two people or two hundred, these skills will give you something solid to stand on.

Nerves will come. They always do. But you can step forward knowing that you're not alone and that the words will come when you need them most.

Understanding Nerves: What's Really Happening

Long before I learned how to lead meetings, run presentations, or record myself with confidence, I struggled each time I had to speak up. My body would betray me first: my heart racing, my hands trembling, my thoughts scattering. I felt like my own body was working against me, but over time, I realized that those reactions were not failures. They were signals.

When we anticipate speaking in front of others, our brain triggers what's known as the "fight or flight" response. In that moment, your amygdala senses a threat. It tells your hypothalamus to activate the sympathetic nervous system. That, in turn, signals your adrenal glands to release adrenaline (also known as epinephrine).[5] Adrenaline floods your bloodstream, speeds up your heart, increases your breathing rate, redirects blood to major muscle groups, tightens muscles, dries your mouth, sharpens senses. It is your body preparing for what it perceives as a threat, even if that threat is simply a group of people listening to you.

Nerves are not a sign that you are weak or unprepared. They are your body's natural response to stepping outside your comfort zone. Those butterflies in your stomach can become the very energy that makes your words more powerful when you learn to work with them.

In the field of public speaking, experts often point to this physiology to explain why well-prepared speakers still feel so much tension. Researcher Alison Wood Brooks at Harvard found that when speakers reframe the physical signs of nerves: the racing heart, sweaty palms — as excitement instead of fear, their delivery improves significantly.[6]

Understanding this changed how I approached those moments. I stopped fighting my body and started listening to it. I began to see my nerves as reminders that the moment mattered.

When I faced high stress in that setting, my mouth dried, my pulse pounded, and my mind tried to flee. But I began to rely on small practices — deep breathing, intentional focus, anchoring my mind on one clear idea — that helped me stay present. Over time, I saw how structure and presence quieted the noise of the nerves.

One insight I've noticed repeatedly is that nerves tend to peak right before we speak, then fade once we begin. It is like standing at the edge of a pool. The water looks cold, but when you dive in, your body adjusts, and the shock lessens. You get into your rhythm. The same thing happens with voice and speech. Those first few sentences may feel shaky, but once you begin, your voice gains its flow.

Recognizing this has helped me push past freeze mode. I learned to accept the shaking, to take controlled breaths, to lean into structure rather than perfection. I remind myself that if my heart is pounding, it is because something is happening. If my voice feels shaky, it's the body's attempt to respond.

One final reality: prolonged stress or repeated unease (when left unmanaged) can become harmful because the body stays in high gear too long. That is why learning how to calm, ground, and steady yourself when nerves rise becomes not just helpful, but necessary.

Accepting your nerves doesn't mean letting them control you. It means acknowledging what's happening in your body, grounding yourself, and then speaking anyway. Some of the best speakers in the world still get nervous before stepping on stage. The difference is that they've learned how to ride the wave instead of letting it knock them down.

So the next time you feel your heart race, your jaw clench, your mouth go dry, remember this is not failure. It is your system sending a warning and preparing you. Take a deep breath, center yourself, and step forward. Your body may tremble at first, but your voice will grow stronger through it. Nerves are not your enemy. They are proof that your voice matters.

[5] *Harvard Health Publishing*, "Understanding the Stress Response," Harvard Medical School, updated July 6, 2020.
[6] Alison Wood Brooks, "Get Excited: Reappraising Pre-Performance Anxiety as Excitement," Journal of Experimental Psychology: General, Vol. 143, No. 3 (2014): 1144–1158.

Shifting Focus: It's Not About You

No matter how much preparation I do, there are always moments when my nerves try to get the best of me. It happens right before I step into a meeting, before I share my opinion in a group, or even when I am about to give a short presentation. My heart starts to race. My hands feel slightly damp. My mind moves faster than my words. In those moments, it is not about pretending that the fear is not there. It is about managing it so that my voice can still come through.

One of the first things I learned is the power of the breath. Nerves often make us breathe shallowly, which tightens the throat and makes speaking harder. I now make it a habit to pause, take a slow, deep breath, and let it out gently before I begin. This simple action calms my body and signals to my mind that I am safe. It slows my heartbeat and clears my head just enough to focus. Sometimes I take two or three breaths if the nervous energy feels intense. Breathing does not erase the nerves, but it creates space for me to gather myself.

Another technique that has helped me is grounding through the senses. When my thoughts start to spiral, I bring my attention to something concrete in the room. It could be the texture of my pen, the weight of my feet on the floor, or the sound of my breath. By focusing on the present moment, I remind myself that I am not in danger. I am simply about to speak. This small act pulls me out of the storm in my head and anchors me in reality.

One of the most powerful ways to calm your nerves is to shift the spotlight away from yourself and toward the audience. When we make it all about *us* — our fear, our accent, our clothes, our mistakes — the pressure builds until it feels unbearable. But the truth is, no one is really there for you. Apart from maybe your mom showing up to cheer you on, people did not come to watch you. They came for themselves. They came to learn something, to be inspired, to get a new perspective. Once you understand that, the weight on your shoulders begins to lift.

Your audience isn't there to judge what you wear or how you look. They are there to learn, to be inspired, and to gain something meaningful from what you say. That realization changes everything. You need to stop worrying about impressing people and start focusing on *serving* them.

It's not about putting on a perfect performance. It's about showing up with sincerity and purpose. This is where a simple but effective technique comes in, especially in those early days when you are still getting comfortable. Just like in small settings, pick one friendly face in the audience. It could be someone nodding, smiling, or simply looking attentive. Keep returning your gaze to that person whenever nerves start to rise. If everyone looks intimidating, pick one person and imagine they are your supporter. Some speakers even say to pick an "unfriendly" face to practice not taking it personally and to keep their focus steady.

As I mentioned before, speaking is like lifting weights. You do not start by lifting a hundred pounds.

You begin with one, then five. The same is true for managing your nerves. Start small. Focus on one friendly face, and use that moment of calm to ground yourself as you continue with your speech.

These techniques may seem small, but together they form a powerful toolkit. Managing nerves is not about eliminating them entirely. Even the most experienced speakers feel their hearts pound before stepping on stage. The difference is that they have learned to channel that energy instead of being controlled by it. Breath, grounding, reframing, pausing, and faith all work together to steady your voice.

If you are reading this and nerves often hold you back, I want you to know that it is possible to work with them. Start with one technique. Maybe it is taking a deep breath before you speak. Maybe it is writing a short phrase that reminds you of your worth and repeating it silently. Over time, as you practice, you will begin to notice shifts. Your voice will come out clearer. Your thoughts will settle more quickly. You will start to trust yourself in the moment.

And most importantly, remember: you get one chance at this life. Do not turn it into a mental circus where you tear yourself apart. The audience is not waiting for you to fail. They are waiting to hear what you have to say. Shift the light off yourself, anchor into your message, and give them your best.

Structuring Your Message

One of the most powerful ways to reduce nerves and boost clarity is to have a clear structure. When you know exactly where you're going, your mind has less room to panic, and your audience can follow your message easily. Over time, I learned that the strongest speeches, whether long or short, usually follow a simple rhythm, what MIT professor Patrick Winston described as: Introduction, Body, and Conclusion.[7]

Think of it this way:

★ Tell them what you're going to say.
★ Say it.
★ Tell them what you just said.

When I stand to speak, I begin by setting the tone with a strong opening. I call this the empowerment promise: the moment where you tell your audience what they will walk away with. It's not about impressing anyone with big words or complicated phrases. It's about making it clear why they should listen and what value they'll receive by the end. That clarity grounds me. It keeps my nerves in check because I know exactly why I'm there and what I need to deliver. It also gives the audience a reason to lean in.

Once the message has been introduced, the middle is where the heart of it lives. This is where I unpack the main idea, clear up confusion, and bring the message into focus. A helpful way to do this is by first clarifying what your message is *not* about. This step removes distractions and helps your audience stay aligned. Then, move naturally into your main points, building each one with intention.

When I have a lot to say but only a short time to speak, I scan my thoughts quickly and pull out the key points that truly matter. I put them in order of importance, making sure that the most essential ones come first. That way, if time runs out or things shift unexpectedly, the core message is still delivered. For example, if I were explaining the dynamics of a car engine, I would list everything I want to say, then arrange the list so that the two most important ideas are at the top. Even if I only had a few minutes, the audience would still walk away with the essence of what they need to know.

This approach has saved me many times. There have been moments when the time for my speech was cut in half without warning. Instead of panicking, I was able to adjust smoothly because my thoughts were structured. I could jump to the conclusion naturally, without losing the thread of my message. That kind of flexibility doesn't come from memorizing a script word for word. It comes from understanding the skeleton of your message so well that you can build around it, no matter the situation.

The closing is just as important as the opening. I make it a point to end by circling back to my main idea, reminding the audience of what I promised at the beginning. This repetition isn't about sounding redundant. It's about reinforcing the key takeaways so they stick. Most people remember the first and last things they hear, so I use the ending to give the message weight. I want people to walk away clear, not confused.

Structuring your message in this way isn't just about impressing your audience. It's about empowering yourself. When your message is clear, your mind is calmer. Your delivery becomes more confident because you're not scrambling to remember what comes next. You know your direction, and that steadiness transfers to your audience.

Over time, this structure becomes second nature. Whether I'm giving a presentation, answering a question in a meeting, or sharing my testimony in church, the rhythm is the same. Introduce the message clearly. Develop it with purpose. Conclude by reinforcing the heart of it.

I encourage you to practice this structure in your daily conversations. Use it the next time you explain an idea to a colleague, share a thought in a group, or even tell a story to a friend. Notice how it keeps you focused and makes your words more impactful. With practice, structuring your message no longer feels like a technique but becomes a natural way to speak with power and clarity.

---

[7] Winston, Patrick. *"How to Speak."* Massachusetts Institute of Technology (MIT OpenCourseWare), 2018. Available at:
https://www.youtube.com/watch?v=Unzc731iCUY

Reflection: Turning Fear Into Focus

Take a deep breath. Think back to the last time you had to speak in front of others. A meeting, a classroom, a party, or even a family gathering. What did you feel at that moment? Maybe your hands trembled, your heart raced, or your thoughts scattered. Those feelings are not weak. They are reminders that you care about what you are doing.

Managing nerves is not about eliminating fear; it is about learning how to work through it. In the same way muscles grow through resistance, your voice grows stronger through moments of discomfort. Every time you stand up to speak, even if your words shake, you are building endurance. You are reminding yourself that you can do demanding things.

Now take a moment to think about your message. What do you want people to remember when you speak? If you could leave your audience with one truth, one lesson, one simple encouragement... what would it be? That's your empowerment promise. When you focus on that, your nerves begin to settle because the spotlight shifts from you to your purpose.

Here's a simple exercise to help you turn fear into focus. The next time you are preparing to speak (it doesn't matter how small the audience), write down your message into three short parts:

1. What do you want to promise your audience?
2. How will you deliver that promise?

117

3. How will you remind them of it at the end?

Once you have it written down, practice saying it aloud. You can do it in front of a mirror or record yourself. Or even talk it through with a friend. Listen not for perfection, but for truth. Do your words sound honest? Do they sound like you? Adjust as you go, and remember: your audience doesn't need perfect. They need *real*.

And when you finally step up to speak, look for one friendly face in the room. Focus there. Speak to that person as if you were sharing something meaningful over coffee. If everyone seems serious or distracted, imagine one friendly face. Sometimes that's all you need to steady yourself.

If fear still lingers, whisper a short prayer before you begin. Ask God to speak through you. Remind yourself that He is with you just as He was with Moses. You are not alone in your trembling. You are guided. And when your words begin to flow, that guidance will meet you right where you are.

Afterward, take time to reflect. How did it feel to use your voice this time? What worked? What would you do differently? I encourage you to write it down. Over time, you'll start to notice that what once made you nervous now excites you.

Confidence doesn't come all at once. It grows little by little, in every word you dare to speak. So keep speaking. Keep showing up. And keep giving yourself permission to learn.

CHAPTER 7

Speaking In Meetings, Presentations, And Crowds

Every time you open your mouth to speak, you step into a form of leadership. It doesn't matter if it's a meeting at work, a presentation in front of your team, or a microphone in your hand at church. The moment you speak, you have a chance to influence, encourage, and guide others.

This chapter is all about carrying the courage you've built in smaller spaces into larger ones. When the room grows and the eyes multiply, it can feel like the nerves rush back. But those nerves don't mean you're not ready. They mean you care. They stir a part of you that knows just how powerful your words are.

Speaking in bigger settings is not about being perfect or trying to impress anyone. It's about being prepared, being grounded, and remembering that your voice has value. Every meeting, every presentation, every crowd is just another version of the same thing you've already practiced: showing up and sharing something that matters.

When you stand to speak, your presence communicates before your words do. People don't just hear what you say, they feel how you say it. They feel your calm, your conviction, your belief in what you're sharing. And that comes from knowing why you are there. You are not there to perform. You are there to serve.

So before you step into that meeting or onto that stage, take a deep breath and remind yourself: this isn't about me. It's about what I'm here to give. That one mindset shift can turn fear into focus.

Confidence does not appear when the room grows; it is built through every smaller moment that came before. Every time you shared an idea, asked a question, or practiced your message in private, you were preparing for this.

In this chapter, we're going to talk about how to prepare for those bigger rooms. How to manage your mindset, organize your message, and keep your peace when the spotlight finds you. We'll talk about what it means to show up fully and to let your voice carry. You've been practicing all along. This is just another space for your voice to grow stronger.

The Dynamics of a Meeting

Imagine walking into a meeting room. The air is calm but charged with quiet focus. Chairs scrape softly against the floor as people settle in. Someone flips open a laptop; another checks their notes. There's that faint hum of small talk before the real conversation begins. You take your seat, heart thumping just a little faster than usual, and you glance around the table.

Every person in that room carries something: opinions, expectations, maybe even doubts. And yet, right there in that ordinary moment, you have an opportunity. This isn't just another meeting. It's a space where you can contribute, connect, and influence.

The truth is, meetings are one of the most common places where our voices shrink. We second-guess our ideas. We worry about saying the wrong thing or about how senior leaders might perceive us. But when you prepare with intention, something shifts. You move from silent observer to confident participant.

Before any meeting, take a few minutes to ground yourself. Look at the agenda, even if it's brief. Ask yourself: What is the goal of this discussion? Where might my insight be useful? Write down two or three key ideas or points you'd like to share. You're walking in with purpose.

It also helps to anticipate questions. Think about what others might ask or challenge, especially if you're presenting an update or a proposal. The more you rehearse possible questions in your mind, the calmer you'll feel when they actually arise. At the core, preparation isn't about having all the answers—it's about giving your voice a foundation to stand on.

Once you're in the room, remember that contribution looks different for everyone. You don't have to speak first or the most. You just have to add value. A powerful way to do that is by summarizing what others have said before adding your perspective. For example: "That's a great point, and I'd like to build on it by suggesting..."

This simple habit shows confidence, clarity, and teamwork all at once. Another approach is asking insightful questions. Try questions like, "How does this align with our main goal?" or "What might we be overlooking?" A good question can guide a conversation more effectively than a long comment.

Now, let's talk about hierarchy. Sometimes the reason we stay quiet is not because we lack ideas, but because we feel intimidated by titles. When senior leaders are in the room, it's easy to think your words carry less weight. But the truth is, they invited you to that meeting for a reason. You bring a perspective no one else has. So, speak from that place.

When you do, stay grounded in humility, but don't shrink. Look at the person you're speaking to, project your voice clearly, and speak with calm assurance. Remember that respect goes both ways: your voice deserves to be heard just as much as anyone else's.

Preparation, presence, and participation. These are the three dynamics that shape how you show up in meetings. They help you move from silence to contribution, from uncertainty to influence. The next time you enter a meeting, try to see it differently. It's not a test. It's a training ground. A place to refine your confidence, sharpen your communication, and practice leadership in action. You don't have to dominate the room. Just show up with preparation, speak with intention, and trust that your voice is enough.

Presentations: From Notes to Presence

The room quiets down. You can hear the faint shuffle of papers, a cough, a chair creaking in the corner. Maybe there's a projector humming, or the soft sound of people adjusting in their seats. You look around, and for a brief second, every eye is on you.

That moment can feel heavy, but it's also sacred. Because in that space, you have the power to inform, to inspire, and to move others toward something greater. There's a shift that happens when you move from meetings to presentations. In meetings, you're one voice among many. In a presentation, your voice leads the room. The focus is on you, but the message is not about you: it's about what you're giving.

Before any presentation, ask yourself this: Am I here to inform or to persuade?

If your goal is to inform, your job is to share knowledge clearly. To help people understand, see, or learn.

If your goal is to persuade, then you're inviting them to take action. To help them feel something and believe something enough to move forward. To act.

Understanding this difference changes how you prepare. Informative presentations need structure. Persuasive presentations need heart. The best ones blend both.

One of the most powerful ways to bridge that gap is through storytelling. Stories connect data to emotion. They turn facts into meaning. You can present numbers all day long, but when you add a story — a moment, a person, a real example — people remember. Think about Jesus' parables: He taught us deep truths through simple stories because, in the end, stories reach where statistics cannot.

So when you prepare your next presentation, ask yourself, "What story can I tell that brings this to life?" It doesn't have to be long. Just a short moment that helps your audience see themselves in what you're saying.

Data also has its place. Numbers give your message weight. Use them carefully to build trust and credibility. Visuals, too, can turn complex ideas into something memorable. A good image, graph, or even a keyword on a slide can speak volumes when used with intention. But the heart of a presentation is not your slides or your notes. It's you. It's the way you speak, the tone of your voice, the pace you set, and the peace you bring into the room.

Timing and pacing are crucial. Take your time with your words. Let your audience catch up to your thoughts. Silence is not your enemy: it's your partner. A short pause gives people room to absorb what you just said. It also gives you a moment to breathe, to recenter, and to stay connected.

And remember: how you start and how you end matter most. Your opening should catch attention right away. Begin with a question, a story, a bold statement. Or even a surprising fact. You need something that brings people closer to you. Then, as you move toward your conclusion, circle back. Remind your audience of what they've gained or what you promised. That full-circle moment is what makes your message stick.

When you have a lot to say but not much time, learn to scan your notes and identify your main points. Ask yourself, "If I only had two minutes to speak, what would I want them to remember?" Place your most important points at the top so that even if time runs out, your message still lands.

Rehearsal is also essential. Don't just read your notes silently. Speak them out loud. Practice your transitions, your opening lines, and your closing statement until they feel like second nature. Record yourself, watch it back, and listen not only to your words but to your energy. Are you rushing? Are you connecting? Do you sound like you believe what you're saying? The more you listen, the more you will grow aware of your tone and your presence.

When I prepare for any presentation, I start with the basics. I make sure I am well-presented. I think about what I will wear and how it reflects respect for the moment. I keep my clothes professional, not distracting because I want my message to shine more than my outfit. I also prepare questions ahead of time, especially if I am part of a high-level discussion, like when I was selected to attend a State Bank CEO meeting. I asked in advance why I was chosen and what was expected of me. That helped me feel grounded.

Before any major talk, I always take time to research my audience. Who are they? What are their challenges, hopes, and expectations? What do they need from me? When you understand that, your words become sharper and more compassionate. You stop speaking *at* people and start speaking *to* them.

Every word you speak should bring value. Every message should leave people a little better, a little stronger, or a little more hopeful than before. That is what makes a presentation powerful. It is not the applause at the end, but the quiet change you help create in someone's heart.

And through all of it, remind yourself: the goal is not perfection. The goal is presence. People don't remember flawless speakers; they remember authentic ones. They remember how you made them feel.

So, the next time you find yourself standing before a room, whether it's five people or fifty, take a deep breath. Look for one friendly face. Speak with calm confidence.

★ You have done the work.
★ Now let your presence carry the rest.

Facing a Crowd

Standing before a crowd can feel like standing at the edge of a wave. All of that quiet chatter, the lights, the subtle hum of anticipation. It can all feel larger than life. But that's exactly where your growth lives. The crowd isn't there to scare you; it's there to stretch you.

When you speak to a crowd, whether it's in a church, a conference, or a community event, the first thing to remember is this: people don't expect perfection. They expect value. They came to hear something that will help them learn, grow, or see themselves more clearly. That's it. They're not sitting there with a scorecard, waiting to catch your mistakes. They're waiting for something real.

When you stop chasing perfection, you start giving value. You focus less on sounding right and more on being present. You speak from your heart, not your fear.

Crowds are simply made up of individuals, each one looking for a reason to connect with what you're saying. Your job is to find that connection and nurture it.

One way to do that is through energy. The larger the room, the more energy you need to project. You don't have to shout, but you do need to fill the space with your presence. Imagine your words reaching the back of the room and wrapping around the last person in the last row. Let your body express the same energy that's in your words. Use your hands, your posture, your facial expressions. Movement keeps the audience's attention, but it also helps release your own nervous energy.

Your voice is your instrument. Use it with range and rhythm. Don't speak in a single volume: it flattens your message. Instead, let your voice rise when you're emphasizing something powerful and soften when you want to draw people in. A good speaker knows that silence is just as important as speech. A pause can make people lean in. It gives your words time to breathe and your audience time to absorb.

Think of a pause like punctuation in music. It's what makes the melody come alive.

Another key skill is reading the room. Because great speakers are also great observers. Notice the body language in front of you: are people leaning in or checking their phones? Are their faces curious, confused, or distant? Adjust your tone accordingly. If you feel your energy dipping, ask a question, share a short story, or invite engagement.

The best presentations are conversations, not monologues. So every time you step up to speak, see it as a conversation, not a show. Your words are the bridge between you and the people in front of you. Some will nod, some will stay quiet, some may even look distant...

but that's all right. Every person receives in their own way. Your job is not to control how they listen. It's to keep showing up and giving your best.

And when you feel nerves creeping in, remind yourself: no one came to judge. You are not here to prove something. You're here to share something. No one came to critique your outfit or count your pauses. They came to find meaning for themselves. Maybe they're searching for inspiration, guidance, or even just comfort in hearing someone speak truthfully. So take the light off yourself. Focus on them. Because confidence doesn't mean never feeling fear, it means trusting your preparation and your purpose more than the fear itself.

Your purpose is to give. When you think of your speech as a gift rather than a test, your words naturally flow with ease and confidence.

Faith and Focus

Before every big moment, I take a quiet pause. Sometimes it's just one deep breath, sometimes a whisper of a prayer. I remind myself that I am not walking into the room alone. Because the truth is, none of us speaks alone.

When you walk into a meeting, a stage, or a crowd, God walks in with you. He equips you for every space He places you in. You are not there by accident. If

He opened the door, He already knows you can carry the message meant for that moment.

Faith helps quiet the noise inside your mind. The doubts, the comparisons, the what-ifs: they lose their power when you trust that your presence has purpose. You don't have to control the outcome; you just have to show up with obedience and honesty.

I've learned that when I prepare my heart as much as my notes, everything changes. There's a calm that comes from knowing it's not all on my shoulders. My job is to speak with truth and intention; God's job is to make sure the message lands where it needs to. That little moment of surrender brings focus. It takes the light off of me and places it back where it belongs: on the purpose of the message.

Faith also gives perspective. When you believe that every space is a part of your preparation, you stop rushing to the next one. You start seeing growth in the process itself. Even the small, quiet rooms become sacred training grounds.

And focus? It's the partner of faith. When you focus, you silence distractions. You listen to the room, you connect to your breath, you keep your mind where your feet are. Faith reminds you *why* you're there; focus keeps you present *while* you're there.

There's peace in that balance: trusting God with the big picture while staying attentive to the moment in front of you. So before you speak next time, pause. Take a breath. Remember that the same God who gave you the voice will also guide it. You don't have to be perfect or powerful. You just have to be present, faithful, and willing.

Because when you speak from that place (from faith and focus combined), your words don't just fill the room. They reach hearts.

Reflection: Speaking with Focus and Purpose

Before your next meeting or presentation, take a quiet moment for yourself. Maybe close your eyes. Breathe. Instead of asking, *What if I mess up?* try asking, *What if this moment was designed just for me?*

So often, we walk into rooms thinking everyone's watching us, waiting for perfection. But that is not true. People are not there to judge. They are there to listen, to learn, and to find something in your words that connects with them. You are not performing for them. You are serving them. When you shift your focus from fear to purpose, the pressure begins to fade.

I have learned to remind myself that I am not walking into any room alone. Whether it is a board meeting, a classroom, or a crowded event, I carry something greater within me. God walks in with me. That small reminder brings peace to my spirit every single time. I might still feel my heart race or my palms sweat, but I know I have been equipped for that moment. I do not have every answer. I just have to be present and willing.

When you let go of the need to prove yourself, you begin to notice more. You notice the faces in front of you. You sense the energy in the room. You remember that it is not about performance. It is about purpose. Every person listening is looking for something: clarity, inspiration, a spark of courage. Your role is simply to give what you have with honesty and intention.

After each speaking moment, take time to reflect, not to judge yourself but to learn. Sometimes the smallest moments reveal the biggest growth. Maybe you spoke a little slower than usual and felt calmer, or you made eye contact and saw someone smile back. Those small details matter. They are signs of progress. Because growth does not happen all at once. It builds quietly, through these little steps of courage.

Every time you speak, whether it is to two people or two hundred, you are strengthening your voice. You are learning how to connect, how to stand in your truth.

Sometime this week, choose one small speaking opportunity. It could be a meeting, a short presentation, or even a family discussion. Before it begins, take a few moments to center yourself. Sit quietly, place a hand on your heart, and remind yourself that you are equipped for this. You do not need to have all the right words; you only need to show up with honesty and intention. Remind your heart that you are not alone. Remind your mind that your worth does not depend on perfect delivery. Remind your spirit that you were chosen for this moment for a reason.

And when you open your mouth, speak from that place. Steady and full of purpose. You will be amazed how different it feels when you stop worrying about being perfect and start trusting that you were meant to be there.

After you speak, grab your journal and write about the experience. What did you notice about your tone, your energy, your connection with others? Did you feel nervous at first? Did that feeling change as you began to speak? What surprised you?

Then, end your reflection with gratitude. Thank yourself for showing up. Thank your voice for doing what it was made to do. Thank God for walking beside you through every word.

This simple act of reflection will help you track your growth in real time. Each time you write, you will see how your courage expands and your voice grows stronger. It is a quiet kind of transformation, but it is real, and it starts here: with one voice, one moment, and one choice to speak.

CHAPTER 8

Speaking Beyond Work: Finding Your Voice In Life

For most of my early twenties, I thought speaking up was something I only had to do at work. Presentations, meetings, interviews... That was where I needed to sound confident. But I realized something over time. The way I use my voice outside of work matters even more. The tone I use with my family, how I speak to my friends, and even how I talk to myself all reflect who I really am.

Speaking beyond work is about carrying that same confidence, clarity, and grace into your everyday life. It is about learning to use your voice in ways that strengthen your relationships instead of creating distance. Sometimes, that means having an honest conversation with someone you love. Other times, it means saying no when you usually say yes.

When I began to pay attention to how I spoke in my personal life, I noticed small but powerful changes. At work, I prepared before meetings so I could speak clearly. At home, I learned to pause before reacting. The more I practiced patience and intentional speech, the more peace I felt in my relationships. I stopped trying to

135

be right all the time and started focusing on being understood.

Many of us struggle with this. We think silence keeps the peace, but often, silence creates space for misunderstanding. We hold back because we do not want to offend anyone or cause conflict, but what ends up happening is that people cannot see where our hearts truly are. They guess. They assume. And that creates even more distance.

Finding your voice beyond work is not about being louder. It is about being honest, even when it feels uncomfortable. It is about expressing yourself with kindness, so your words bring healing instead of hurt. When you start speaking up with love and respect, you will notice how much lighter you feel. Communication stops being a battle and becomes a bridge.

In this chapter, we will talk about what it means to use your voice in your everyday life: with your family, your friends, and the people closest to you. You will see that confidence is not something that belongs only in boardrooms or on stages. It belongs in your kitchen, in your living room, in the way you talk to your children, your partner, and even the way you pray.

By the time you finish this chapter, my hope is that you will see your voice differently. You will understand that using it is not just a skill. It is an act of love.

Speaking truthfully, gently, and with faith allows you to bring peace where there was once confusion, and closeness where there was once distance.

The Home as Your First Audience

Before we learn to speak confidently to the world, we learn to speak at home. The people closest to us become our first audience. They are the ones who see our raw emotions, our habits, and our silences. And because they see us without the filters we use outside, they often reveal how we truly communicate.

There was a time in my life when silence felt safer than honesty. I thought that by staying quiet, I was keeping the peace. But silence can build invisible walls, and before we know it, those walls separate us from the people we love. I learned that communication is not just about words. It is about courage. It takes courage to say, "I need help," "I'm hurt," or even, "I love you." It takes courage to show up truthfully.

That season of learning taught me that love is not proven through silence or sacrifice alone. It is proven through openness. When we speak from a place of compassion, even when it feels uncomfortable, we create room for healing. Speaking up with grace can be one of the most loving things we ever do.

Now I see communication as a meaningful act. It is not something we do only in meetings or with microphones. It is something we practice daily with our partners, our children, our friends, and even with ourselves. Every conversation is a small chance to bring more understanding into the world.

When I speak to someone I care about, I remind myself to slow down. To listen before I respond. To speak not just to be heard, but to connect. I notice the tone of my voice because tone is the bridge between my intention and how my words are received. A gentle tone can carry a difficult truth farther than a loud one ever could.

If you are reading this, I want you to pause for a moment and think about your own home, your own relationships. Who are the people that make up your first audience? Who do you speak to every day... and how do you speak to them? Are your conversations filled with honesty or with hesitation? Do you listen with patience, or are you already preparing your reply before they finish?

These reflections are not meant to make you feel guilty. They are an invitation to become aware. Because awareness is where change begins. Once we notice how we communicate, we can begin to shape it with intention.

Start small. Maybe this week you can choose one person (a family member, a close friend, or even a coworker) and make a decision to speak with more clarity and kindness. It could be a short conversation where you express gratitude, share how you truly feel, or apologize if something has been left unsaid. Watch what happens when you bring honesty and empathy into the room.

You can also practice by journaling. Write down one relationship that feels tense or distant and ask yourself: *What have I been holding back from saying? What am I afraid might happen if I say it?*

Then, pray about it. Ask God to guide your words and soften your heart before you speak. Sometimes the right words come not from rehearsing, but from being still enough to listen.

Remember that, in most cases, your home is your first stage, and also your safest one. This is where you can make mistakes, learn, and try again. Every time you choose to speak truthfully instead of retreating into silence, you strengthen your voice. Every conversation becomes a rehearsal for the kind of communicator you want to be.

Friendships and Social Spaces

Outside of work and home, we find ourselves in spaces that shape who we are becoming. For me, that space was often my church. It was more than just a building. It was a community – a place where I learned the power of communication in all its forms: speaking with care, listening with empathy, offering guidance, and showing quiet support through presence alone.

Over time, I realized that people were watching me more than I knew. Younger women would come to me with questions, ask for advice, or quietly observe how I handled things. They listened to what I said, yes, but they also paid attention to what I did. It reminded me that leadership doesn't always come with a title. Sometimes, it simply comes from the example you set when others are watching.

You may not always feel comfortable with attention. There will be moments when you wonder if you are setting the right example or saying the right thing. There may even be times when you feel pressure to impress others just to belong. But remember this: influence is not about perfection. It is about authenticity. The people around you do not need you to be flawless; they need to see that faith, kindness, and courage can exist even within imperfection. Speaking with intention can bring comfort to someone who is hurting or encouragement to someone who is doubting herself. And sometimes, it is not about giving advice at all. It is about showing up, listening, and letting your words reflect compassion.

Friendships and social spaces become places to practice using our voice. They become spaces where we laugh, unwind, and share our lives with others. But even here, confidence and authenticity matter.

Friendships are where we learn the balance between speaking and listening. When you speak, do so from a place of care. When you listen, do it fully, without planning your response in your head. There's a calm power in simply being present for someone. They are also a safe space to test your voice, to learn when to speak up and when to listen. You might say the wrong thing sometimes or misread a moment, but that's okay. Because we are not looking for perfection, we are looking for growth. For confidence.

And this means... Growing in confidence is learning to express your needs and boundaries with grace. This can feel uncomfortable at first, especially if you're used to keeping the peace or saying yes to everything. But saying no kindly is one of the most loving things you can do for yourself and for others. A gentle "I can't make it this time" or "I need a bit of space right now" doesn't make you a bad friend. It makes you an honest person. Healthy relationships are built on truth, not guilt.

You can also use your voice to encourage others. When you notice someone doing something well, say it out loud. A simple compliment or word of affirmation can go a long way. We often underestimate how powerful our words can be in someone's day. If you see a friend trying something new or stepping out of their comfort zone, let them know you're proud of them. Confidence is contagious, and encouragement multiplies it.

Take a moment and think about your own spaces. Who looks up to you, even quietly? How do you show up for them? Are your conversations life-giving? Do your words reflect the kind of person you're striving to become?

You don't have to be a preacher or a public speaker to make an impact. You can lead through your everyday actions. Maybe this week, try one simple act of communication that brings light to someone else. It could be sending a kind message, calling a friend you've lost touch with, or speaking honestly in a moment when it would be easier to stay quiet.

The truth is, social spaces give us daily opportunities to practice connection, empathy, and influence. The way we communicate in these small circles shapes how we speak in bigger ones. So start where you are. Speak with kindness and with grace.

The Ripple Effect of Your Voice

I have always believed that our words carry power. They have the power to mend or to break, to heal or to wound. The older you grow, the more you will see how one phrase can change the atmosphere in a room. Your words have the power to move someone from doubt to action, to lift them out of a difficult season, and even to change the direction of their life. In the same way, negative words can hold someone back. They can cause a person to remain mentally trapped in pain or fear. That is the true ripple effect of your voice.

When you speak with compassion, your words become a source of healing. They remind others that they are not alone, that someone stands with them in their pain or uncertainty. You let them know that mistakes don't make them unworthy and that growth is still possible. Sometimes, compassion isn't about fixing anything. It's about saying, "I see you. I hear you. I'm with you." That simple acknowledgment can begin healing what silence or misunderstanding once broke.

There were seasons in my life when conversations brought restoration more than any apology ever could. A soft word in a tense moment can turn the direction of a relationship. It reminds me of Proverbs 15:1 (NIV): "A gentle answer turns away wrath, but a harsh word stirs up anger." You don't need to be a perfect speaker to do this. You only need to use your voice with care and intention, to choose words that bring clarity, comfort, and restoration instead of confusion or harm. Sometimes, it begins with something as simple as taking a breath and allowing your words to create calm rather than turmoil.

I also believe there is something deeply spiritual about communication. Every word we speak leaves a trace, not just in the atmosphere, but in the heart of a person who hears it. God listens to the way we speak to His people. Our words can become ministry in constant motion, healing as they are uttered. You don't have to be standing at a pulpit to deliver a message that heals. You could be on the phone, at work, or standing in your kitchen, and your voice can still carry love, hope, and grace.

I think about the small ways God uses our voices every day: a kind word to a stranger, a prayer spoken aloud, or a gentle encouragement shared in passing.

You may never see how far those ripples travel, but someone else will feel them. And that's what matters.

For me, learning to use my voice with purpose has been an act of faith. I pray before I speak, especially when emotions are high. I ask God to help me say what needs to be said and to keep me silent when silence will bring more peace. Some days I get it right, other days I stumble. But I've learned that God can use even my imperfect words for good when they come from a sincere heart.

If you are reading this, I want you to think about the people in your life: your friends, your coworkers, your family. How do your words land when you speak to them? Do they bring calm or chaos? Healing or harm? These questions are about awareness. Once we become aware of how our words move through the world, we can begin to use them with more grace.

Remember: your voice has ripple effects. You might never see how far they go, but God does. Every time you speak life into someone, you plant a seed that can grow long after you're gone. So let your words be intentional. Let them build, not break. Let them lift, not wound. Your voice can be a ministry in motion. Use it well. Speak with love. And trust that even in the smallest conversation, God can use your words to move mountains.

Reflection: The Quiet Influence of Your Own Voice

There is something beautiful about realizing that your words are like seeds. They may seem small when you speak them, but once they land in the soil of someone's heart, they begin to grow. Sometimes the growth is quiet and unseen; sometimes it's vibrant and immediate, but your voice plants something.

Your voice doesn't just fill a room—it lingers. It settles into hearts, it stirs thoughts, and sometimes it even softens wounds you didn't know existed. That realization can feel both humbling and powerful. Your voice does not have to be loud to make an impact. It only has to be aligned with your heart. When you speak with sincerity, when you choose peace over pride, when you let kindness lead before certainty, you become a vessel for healing in ways you might never see.

This week, I want you to simply notice. Notice how your words move through your days. Notice the tone you use with the people you love. Notice the moments when silence feels wiser than speaking. Awareness is the first step toward transformation.

If you feel led, write about it. Not as a task, but as a conversation with yourself. Ask, "What kind of ripple do I want my words to leave behind?"

Every conversation is a form of watering. Every kind word, every moment of listening, every time you pause before reacting—that's you tending the garden of your connections. And just like your flowers, the people in your life respond to the way you care for them. They open up in warmth because the words you speak shape the kind of garden you are growing around you.

So this week, ask yourself: what am I watering with my words? Think about the people closest to you — your family, your friends, your community. These are roots that keep you grounded. Strengthen them with presence, attention, and kindness.

★ Speak softly where the world is harsh.
★ Speak with hope where there is doubt.

Your words are more than sounds; remember, they are seeds.

CHAPTER 9

The Language Beyond Work

Sometimes communication begins long before we speak. You can walk into a room, say nothing at all, and still tell a story. Your body speaks first. Have you ever walked into a room and instantly recognized who was confident, even before they spoke?

There's something about the way certain people carry themselves, the way they meet your eyes, the steadiness in their breathing. They could be completely silent, yet you can sense their confidence. Their assurance.

That's because before you ever speak, your body speaks for you.

Many times, I've seen people focus so much on what to say that they forget *how* they are saying it. They rehearse their points but neglect the posture, the pauses, the gestures that make those points come alive. Yet the truth is simple: people believe your body before they believe your words. You could say all the right things, but if your body is closed off or tense, your message will never land with the same impact.

Your posture, your expression, the way you hold your head... all that sends a message. Communication starts long before you open your mouth. You don't have to be a professional speaker to understand this; you've probably lived it. Maybe you've walked into a meeting trying to disappear into your chair, or maybe you've had days where you stood tall and people seemed to listen differently. That's not a coincidence. That's your body telling your story before you do.

Open hands invite. Crossed arms protect. Small, intentional movements help you express sincerity and passion, while frantic gestures can signal anxiety. The goal isn't to choreograph yourself but to become aware of how your gestures support your message.

So what is your body already saying? Your body language is like the opening line of your message. It sets the tone for everything that follows. You can start simple. Next time you enter a room, take a breath before you walk in. Roll your shoulders back. Lift your chin slightly. Feel your feet grounded on the floor. That tiny pause can change everything. It signals to your mind that you are here with purpose. It tells the room, "I belong here."

As I learned over the years, even when your voice shakes, your body can help carry you. It can steady you when your words feel uncertain. The way you stand, the way you look at your audience, the way you hold yourself — these are all small acts of courage.

Your body is a powerful communicator, and learning how to use it intentionally is one of the easiest ways to build confidence. Standing tall doesn't mean being stiff. It's about alignment (shoulders back, chest open, spine straight, feet planted). When your body is balanced, your voice naturally sounds stronger and your thoughts flow more clearly. You can try it right now as you read this: take a deep breath, straighten up, and notice how different you feel.

This chapter is about this. What happens when your voice meets your body? It's about the quiet power that speaks through your posture, your breath, your eyes, and your presence. Because confidence is not only in what you say… it's also in what you show.

We'll explore how your body carries your message before your words even arrive and how learning to listen to that physical language can change the way you communicate.

And by the end of this chapter, my hope is you'll see that true confidence is not about removing fear but about moving with it.

Nervousness as Energy, Not the Enemy

If there's one truth that every speaker, leader, and teacher eventually learns, it's this: *everyone gets nervous.* The butterflies, the sweaty palms, the quick heartbeat. They don't disappear because you're experienced or talented. They're part of being human.

There was a moment in my own journey when I realized that nervousness wasn't a sign of weakness. I used to pray that the shaking would stop before I spoke, that I could somehow walk to the front of the room calm and steady. But over time, I learned that my nerves weren't working against me. They were reminding me that what I was about to say mattered. They were the body's way of saying, "This is important!"

Once you understand that, *everything* changes. Instead of fighting your nerves, you start to work with them. You breathe through them, direct their energy, and let that energy serve your words.

Think of nervousness like electricity. It can shock you or light the room... it all depends on how you use it. When you fight it, it becomes chaos. And when you channel it, it becomes powerful.

So how do you start doing that?

First, expect it. Don't walk into a presentation or a conversation hoping you'll feel nothing. That hope sets you up for panic the moment nerves appear. Instead, greet them. When you feel that flutter in your stomach or the tightness in your chest, silently tell yourself, *This is energy. This is exciting. My body is getting ready.*

Next, slow down your breathing. Nervous energy lives in shallow breaths. You don't need to hide; you just need to focus. Then, move. Roll your shoulders, shake your hands, or stretch lightly before you speak. Motion helps your body release tension instead of storing it.

You might look around and think that other people don't feel it—that the confident ones are somehow immune to fear. But that's not true. Every person who stands in front of an audience, leads a meeting, or speaks from the heart feels it. The difference is they've learned to endure it. They've learned to move through it instead of running from it. That's what separates fear from courage.

_____

Turning Tension into Presence

Now that you know nervousness isn't your enemy, the next step is learning to turn that tension into presence. The secret is not forcing calm but grounding yourself. Before you speak, take a moment to feel your feet on the floor. Imagine roots growing from them, steadying you. Your breath connects to your body, your faith connects you to something greater. When you combine both, presence happens.

There's power in stillness. When you pause before you begin, when you stand with open posture and calm energy, the room quiets with you. You're no longer reacting to fear… you're leading with peace. With purpose.

You can also anchor your body with small physical cues. Maybe it's pressing your thumb and forefinger together as a reminder to stay focused. Maybe it's exhaling before your first word. Find what grounds you and practice it until it becomes natural.

And if your voice shakes, let it. Your body might tremble, your heart might race, but keep speaking. Every time you endure the nerves and finish your sentence, you're teaching your body that it can handle this. Over time, the fear fades, and what's left is strength.

When you let go of trying to appear perfect, you make room for authenticity. You stop focusing on yourself and start focusing on connection. Because the goal isn't to look unshakable, it's to be honest and open.

So the next time your hands tremble or your heart races, remember this: you are not broken. You are alive. Every beat of that nervous heart is proof that you care, that your message matters, and that you are stepping into something meaningful.

Let your nervousness remind you of your purpose, not your limits. Let it pull you closer to presence, not panic. And when you finish speaking, even if your voice shakes, even if your palms are sweaty, smile. You've done something brave. You've turned fear into faith.

Reflection: Turning Fear into Flow

Confidence doesn't mean silence before courage. It means breathing through the noise inside you. The next time you feel nervous, remember that this is energy. This is the purpose. And let that anchor you in the present moment.

Here's something simple to practice this week:

1. Ground yourself. Before every conversation or meeting, pause and plant your feet firmly. Feel your weight supported.

2. Breathe with intention. Inhale through your nose, hold for two counts, and exhale slowly.

3. Speak from gratitude. Begin each interaction with a quiet thank you: thank you for this moment, this chance, this voice.

Your body will begin to understand that it's safe, that your voice belongs. Over time, nervousness turns into momentum, and momentum turns into presence. Remember the flower story? Growth takes space, light, and a bit of watering every day. Your confidence works the same way. Each time you speak, breathe, and show up (even with shaking hands), you are watering the roots of courage within you.

So go ahead, and step forward again. Speak in the small rooms. Breathe through the nerves. Trust that your body and your voice will find their rhythm together. You don't need to chase perfection. You just need to show up, grounded, open, and ready. Because confidence is not built in the absence of fear. It is built in the gentle rhythm, breath, and practice.

CHAPTER 10

The Moment Before The Leap

There is always a pause before courage: that quiet second when your heart beats faster, your breath catches, and you know something is about to change. That's the moment before the leap. It's the space between staying where you are and stepping into who you are meant to become. Every person who has ever spoken up, led a team, started a business, or shared their truth has faced that same stillness. The nerves, the doubts, the inner voice that says, *What if I fail?* That hesitation doesn't mean you are not ready. It means the leap matters.

This chapter is about that sacred space: the seconds before you act, when fear and faith meet face to face. It's about learning to recognize nervousness not as a barrier, but as a bridge. You'll discover that confidence isn't built by waiting for fear to disappear. It's built by deciding to leap anyway.

We'll talk about how to prepare your heart and your body for those moments. How to pause without freezing. How to pray, breathe, and steady yourself when your mind tells you to retreat. Because speaking up, whether in a meeting, a relationship, or on a stage, always begins with a choice: to step into the unknown with faith that God has already gone ahead of you.

Everyone Is Nervous... But Not Everyone Quits

Imagine a young woman waiting at the back of a conference room. The low murmur of voices fills the air as the audience settles in, moments before she is called to speak. She's gripping her notes a little too tightly, whispering her lines under her breath. In a few seconds, she'll walk out there and speak... and she's terrified.

What she doesn't know is that everyone sitting on the other side of that curtain has been in her place. Every confident speaker, every leader, every person who has ever raised their hand has felt that same heat in their chest. The difference is that some let the fear silence them, and others walk out there anyway.

That's the truth I want you to hold on to: nervousness never goes away completely. It's not something you "outgrow." It's something you work with. Even the most experienced speakers still feel it before they open their mouths. The difference is that they've learned how to endure it.

No matter how long you've been practicing, you will never reach a point where nervousness disappears completely. Even the greatest speakers, leaders, and teachers still feel it before they begin. The difference is, they've stopped fighting it. They've learned to breathe through it, to stand with it, and to let that energy move through their words.

When you start seeing nervousness as energy instead of fear, it becomes something you can use. That rush that feels uncomfortable is actually fuel — it's your body preparing you to perform, to be alert, to connect. The next time your heart starts beating faster, remind yourself: this is readiness. This is my body saying, "You care."

One way to work with nervousness is to give it direction. Before you speak, pause. Let yourself feel your feet against the floor, take a slow breath, and remember that the room is not your enemy. Every person there is looking for something that might help them... They are not focused on your shoes, your outfit, or your accent. They are listening because they want to learn, to grow, to walk away with something new. Once you realize that it's not about you, the pressure eases.

It also helps to picture the moment before speaking as a bridge. On one side stands your fear; on the other, your potential. The trembling doesn't mean you can't cross — it simply means you're human. What matters is taking that first step forward. The act of speaking, of beginning, is what lets fear transform into focus. There's also power in acknowledging that you will make mistakes. Your voice might crack. You might forget a word or lose your place. But those moments don't define you; they make you human. People remember connection, not perfection. The more you allow yourself to be real, the more your message resonates.

If you struggle to calm your nerves, use small grounding rituals. Some people breathe deeply; others silently pray. It takes the focus off me and reminds me that I am only the vessel. The message is what matters.

There are other ways to manage that nervous energy. Move your body before speaking. Stretch your shoulders, unclench your jaw, smile, or hum quietly to warm up your voice. These small movements signal your mind that you're ready. When you walk into a room, make eye contact with one friendly face (maybe someone who looks calm or encouraging), and let that connection anchor you. If you see someone who seems unfriendly, don't get stuck on that. Come back to the friendly face. That person becomes your reminder that you are not alone.

Remember too that every audience, no matter the size, is made up of people... And for the most part, people are kind and forgiving. Most of them are too focused on their own nerves to notice yours. Some might even be silently cheering you on. Everyone wants the speaker to succeed because it makes the experience better for everyone. That's the secret few people talk about: the audience is not judging you. They're hoping you do well.

And if all else fails, remember this truth: you only get one chance at this life. One chance to show up, to speak, to let your story matter. Don't let fear steal that from you. Nervousness will visit you, but it doesn't have to stay. You can thank it for reminding you that this moment matters and then walk forward anyway.

When I first learned this, it changed everything. I realized that the people I admired — the speakers who seemed so calm, so collected — weren't fearless. They had simply learned to stay in motion while being afraid. They had learned that nerves are not a stop sign; they're a signal that you're alive, that something important is unfolding.

You can practice this in small ways. The next time you're about to speak, whether it's in a meeting, a church group, or a conversation with a loved one, notice your body. Notice how the energy rises. Don't try to fight it. Breathe into it, feel it move through you, and then use it. Let it lift your tone, carry your words, and fill your message with sincerity.

Over time, that nervous energy will start to feel familiar. You'll recognize it not as panic, but as purpose. You'll still feel it, but you'll know what to do with it. That's what growth looks like. You don't get rid of the butterflies; you teach them how to fly in formation. So the next time you feel fear bubbling up before you speak, smile a little. You're in the moment before the leap. And that means where you are supposed to be.

Reflection: The Purpose Behind Your Voice

At the end of it all, every voice shakes at first. Every speaker, every leader, every teacher has felt their heart beat a little too fast before saying something that mattered. Nervousness is universal, but it's not a sign of weakness. It's a sign that you care. It's your body's way of reminding you that the moment in front of you is meaningful.

You were never meant to be fearless. You were meant to be brave. There's a difference. Fearless people don't exist. Brave people simply choose to keep going even when their voice trembles.

The purpose of finding your voice isn't to prove you can speak perfectly. It's to share what's real... to bring truth, encouragement, and light into spaces that need it. It's to use your words to build, to connect, and to serve. Your voice is not just for you. It's a tool for healing, for clarity, for leadership, for hope.

Think about your everyday life: the rooms you walk into, the people you meet, the quiet moments where you hesitate before speaking. Those spaces are where your voice belongs. Each one is an invitation. Each one is a place where you can bring something only you have to give.

As you move forward, I want you to remember this: everyone feels nervous, but not everyone steps forward anyway. The difference between silence and speaking up is not confidence. It's willingness.

Willingness to risk, to try, to grow, and to trust that your words have value.

Your voice has been waiting for this... not to sound perfect, but to sound like you. When you speak with sincerity, when you speak from truth, and when you speak with love, you are already enough.

So here's your invitation: Speak. Even if your hands shake. Even if your voice cracks. Even if the words come out softer than you wanted. Because every time you do, you grow a little stronger. Every time you do, you remind yourself and others that courage does not live in the absence of fear: it lives in the decision to rise above it.

Your voice matters, and the world is waiting to hear it.

CONCLUSION

Every time I stand in front of people, I am reminded of something deeper than nerves or confidence. I remember that my voice, and the message within it, matters. These people did not just wander into the room. They chose to be there. They came expecting to hear something that could shift their perspective, even if just a little. That awareness humbles me every time.

It is not about pride or ego. It is not about being seen for the sake of attention. It is about understanding that words have weight and that your voice can be a vessel for something greater. When I speak, I think about what I can leave behind in others, not just for the moment, but for their journey ahead. I want them to leave with a sense of fullness, with a spark of hope or a new understanding that stays with them long after the room empties.

I remind myself that every person sitting there is a reflection of God's creation. Each one carries their own fears, dreams, and silent battles. My responsibility, and yours too, is to speak to that humanity. To speak with care. To use our voices not to impress, but to uplift.

When I stand before others, I pray that my words are more than just mine. I pray that God's voice moves through me. That something I say might light a small flame in someone else's heart. Because when that happens, it is no longer about me. It is about purpose. It is about becoming a vessel of healing, truth, and courage.

And when you use your voice with intention, whether in a meeting, a conversation, a classroom, or a prayer, you are doing more than speaking. You are creating change. You are planting seeds in others, reminding them that they, too, have something valuable to say.

So as you close this book, I want you to remember one thing: your voice is sacred. It carries your experience, your strength, and your faith. Let it move through the world freely. Speak with courage. Speak with love. Speak with purpose.

Because when you do, you will not only change how others hear you. You will change how you hear yourself.

And that is where true freedom begins.